THE MOST IMPORTANT THING

ILLUMINATED

The MOST IMPORTANT THING ILLUMINATED

HOWARD MARKS

ANNOTATED BY
Christopher C. Davis, Joel Greenblatt,
Paul Johnson, and Seth A. Klarman

Uncommon Sense for
the Thoughtful Investor

Columbia Business School
Publishing

Columbia University Press
Publishers Since 1893
New York   Chichester, West Sussex
cup.columbia.edu

Library of Congress Cataloging-in-Publication Data
Marks, Howard, 1946-
The most important thing illuminated : uncommon sense for the thoughtful investor /
Howard Marks.
p. cm.
Includes bibliographical references.
ISBN 978–0–231–16284–5 (cloth : alk. paper)—ISBN 978–0–231–53079–8 (e-book)
1. Investments. 2. Portfolio management. 3. Investment analysis. 4. Risk management.
I. Title.
HG4521.M3215 2012
332.6—dc23
2012003076

Columbia University Press books are printed on permanent and durable acid-free
paper.
This book is printed on paper with recycled content.
Printed in the United States of America

c 10 9 8 7 6

Cover design: Noah Arlow   Book design: Milenda Lee

References to Internet Web sites (URLs) were accurate at the time of writing. Neither
the author nor Columbia University Press is responsible for URLs that may have
expired or changed since the manuscript was prepared.

For Nancy, Jane, and Andrew

With All My Love

Contents

Foreword

For twenty years Howard Marks has been educating investors with his "Memos from the Chairman," and in writing *The Most Important Thing*, Marks drew from these memos to compile the most important lessons he has learned as an investor. That he is an outstanding investor goes without saying; he is also a great teacher and a thoughtful author, and *The Most Important Thing* is a generous gift to all investors.

In *The Most Important Thing Illuminated*, readers will benefit not only from Marks's hard-earned wisdom, but also from the insights of three seasoned investors—Christopher Davis, Joel Greenblatt, and Seth Klarman—and a Columbia Business School adjunct professor, Paul Johnson. Each annotator in this impressive group brings a unique perspective to Marks's work, and an investment style that colors their reaction to Marks's text. For Davis, superior investment ability seems to be innate, and his success is amplified by his commitment to a value approach and his disciplined industry focus. Greenblatt—himself the author of the bestselling investment book *The Little Book That Beats the Market*—has gained tremendous success through his keen eye for irrational institutional behavior. His initial insight into corporate spin-offs has been followed up by his more recent focus on overall market anomalies. Klarman has produced almost three decades of extraordinary results while being aggressively risk adverse—and his performance is even more remarkable when one learns of his near ob-session with down-side protection. Finally, Johnson brings his almost thirty years as an investment professional and twenty years as an adjunct professor to reveal how he has begun to incorporate Marks's wisdom into his courses on security analysis and value investing.

Their annotations on the original text add depth and dimension to Marks's argument, as these four thinkers discuss how Marks's philosophy resonates with, refines, or occasionally differs from their own. Marks even adds his own commentary throughout the text, bringing to light some of the underlying themes that run through the book and articulating the top priorities among his recommended actions. In addition, he offers one extra lesson not covered in the original book, on the importance of reasonable expectations. I like to think of *The Most Important Thing Illuminated* as a surrogate book group with five of the best investment thinkers alive.

Most important, this new project joins *The Most Important Thing* as an invaluable contribution to the value investing canon. Value investing began at Columbia with the publication of Benjamin Graham and David Dodd's *Security Analysis* in 1936. In 2001, the Heilbrunn Center for Graham and Dodd Investing was established at Columbia Business School It has since emerged as the academic home of value investing.

I find it fitting and gratifying that the center played a role in the book's formation. *The Most Important Thing* was initially conceived at CSIMA (the Columbia Student Investment Management Association), Heilbrunn's annual investment conference. After hearing Marks give a presentation at the conference, Myles Thompson, founder of Columbia Business School Publishing, approached him about doing a book based on his memos and his investment philosophy. Marks was enthusiastic about publishing his investment wisdom at the birthplace of value investing and knew his ideas would be embraced by the Heilbrunn community. *The Most Important Thing* was launched a year later at the same event; *The Most Important Thing Illuminated* launched at the 2012 CSIMA meeting.

The Most Important Thing Illuminated continues the value investing community's tradition of generously sharing its ideas, insights, and investment wisdom. The Heilbrunn Center is delighted to be associated with this innovative publication and truly illuminating new contribution.

BRUCE C. GREENWALD
Director, Heilbrunn Center for Graham and Dodd Investing
Robert Heilbrunn Professor of Finance and Asset Management

Introduction

For the last twenty years I've been writing occasional memos to my clients—first at Trust Company of the West and then at Oaktree Capital Management, the company I cofounded in 1995. I use the memos to set forth my investment philosophy, explain the workings of finance and provide my take on recent events. Those memos form the core of this book, and you will find passages from many of them in the pages that follow, for I believe their lessons apply as well today as they did when they were written. For inclusion here I've made some minor changes, primarily to make their message clearer.

> **PAUL JOHNSON:** *I never had a single text to use in teaching my investment courses at the Columbia Graduate School of Business until I read Howard Marks's* The Most Important Thing. *I used his book in the fall of 2011 as the primary text in my course on value investing and security analysis. Marks's discussion was an excellent complement to my lectures.*

What, exactly, is "the most important thing"? In July 2003, I wrote a memo with that title that pulled together the elements I felt were essential for investment success. Here's how it began: "As I meet with clients and prospects, I repeatedly hear myself say, 'The most important thing is X.' And then ten minutes later it's, 'The most important thing is Y.' And then Z, and so on." All told, the memo ended up discussing eighteen "most important things."

Since that original memo, I've made a few adjustments in the things I consider "the most important," but the fundamental notion is unchanged: they're *all* important. Successful investing requires thoughtful attention to many separate aspects, all at the same time. Omit any one and the result is likely to be less than satisfactory. That is why I have built this book around the idea of the most important things—each is a brick in what I hope will be a solid wall, and none is dispensable.

PAUL JOHNSON: *This comment is a theme that runs through* The Most Important Thing *and is critical to Marks's view of investing. I believe the most challenging investment concept to explain to graduate business students is that investing requires the concurrent balancing of many different fundamental issues. The Most Important Thing does an excellent job of making this point clear.*

I didn't set out to write a manual for investing. Rather, this book is a statement of my investment philosophy. I consider it my creed, and in the course of my investing career it has served like a religion. These are the things I believe in, the guideposts that keep me on track. The messages I deliver are the ones I consider the most lasting. I'm confident their relevance will extend beyond today.

HOWARD MARKS: *This book is primarily about what I call "the human side of investing." It does not offer much on financial analysis or investment theory—more how to think and how to deal with the psychological influences that interfere with investment thinking and a lot about the mistakes others make in their thinking. When I say "how to think," I don't mean to suggest that my process is the only way, just one example. You have to follow a disciplined thought process in order to be successful, but it doesn't have to be mine.*

You won't find a how-to book here. There's no surefire recipe for investment success. No step-by-step instructions. No valuation formulas containing mathematical constants or fixed ratios—in fact, very few numbers. Just a way to think that might help you make good decisions and, perhaps more important, avoid the pitfalls that ensnare so many.

It's not my goal to simplify the act of investing. In fact, the thing I most want to make clear is just how complex it is. Those who try to simplify investing do their audience a great disservice. I'm going to stick to general thoughts on return, risk and process; any time I discuss specific asset classes and tactics, I do so only to illustrate my points.

A word about the organization of the book. I mentioned above that successful investing involves thoughtful attention to many areas simultaneously. If it were somehow possible to do so, I would discuss all of them at once. But unfortunately the limitations of language force me to take one topic at a time. Thus I begin with a discussion of the market environment in which investing takes place, to establish the playing field. Then I go on to discuss investors themselves, the elements that affect their investment success or lack of it, and the things they should do to improve their chances. The final chapters are an attempt to pull together both groups of ideas into a summation. Because my philosophy is "of a piece," however, some ideas are relevant to more than one chapter; please bear with me if you sense repetition.

I hope you'll find this book's contents novel, thought provoking and perhaps even controversial. If anyone tells me, "I so enjoyed your book; it bore out everything I've ever read," I'll feel I failed. It's my goal to share ideas and ways of thinking about investment matters that you haven't come across before. Heaven for me would be seven little words: "I never thought of it that way."

In particular, you'll find I spend more time discussing risk and how to limit it than how to achieve investment returns. To me, risk is the most interesting, challenging and essential aspect of investing.

PAUL JOHNSON: The Most Important Thing *is the first comprehensive discussion of risk and its importance in the investment process that I have read. In fact, the strongest aspect of the book and its greatest contribution to the canon of investment wisdom is its extensive discussion of risk.*

When potential clients want to understand what makes Oaktree tick, their number one question is usually some variation on "What have been the keys to your success?" My answer is simple: an effective investment philosophy, developed and honed over more than four decades and implemented conscientiously by highly skilled individuals who share culture and values.

Where does an investment philosophy come from? The one thing I'm sure of is that no one arrives on the doorstep of an investment career with his or her philosophy fully formed. A philosophy has to be the sum of many ideas accumulated over a long period of time from a variety of sources. One cannot develop an effective philosophy without having been exposed to life's lessons. In my life I've been quite fortunate in terms of both rich experiences and powerful lessons.

The time I spent at two great business schools provided a very effective and provocative combination: nuts-and-bolts and qualitative instruction in the pre-theory days of my undergraduate education at Wharton, and a theoretical, quantitative education at the Graduate School of Business of the University of Chicago. It's not the specific facts or processes I learned that mattered most, but being exposed to the two main schools of investment thought and having to ponder how to reconcile and synthesize them into my own approach.

Importantly, a philosophy like mine comes from going through life with your eyes open. You must be aware of what's taking place in the world and of what results those events lead to. Only in this way can you put the lessons to work when similar circumstances materialize again. Failing to do this—more than anything else—is what dooms most investors to being victimized repeatedly by cycles of boom and bust.

SETH KLARMAN: *Keeping your eyes open also increases the probability that you will be prepared for something that has never before occurred. Warren Buffett stressed the importance of this during his search for a successor. Alertness can help to identify and possibly avoid growing risks before it is too late. Marks makes this point in chapter 5.*

I like to say, "Experience is what you got when you didn't get what you wanted."

///

JOEL GREENBLATT: *This is one of my favorite "Howardisms." I have the opportunity to think of it often!*

\\\

Good times teach only bad lessons: that investing is easy, that you know its secrets, and that you needn't worry about risk. The most valuable lessons are learned in tough times. In that sense, I've been "fortunate" to have lived through some doozies: the Arab oil embargo, stagflation, Nifty Fifty stock collapse and "death of equities" of the 1970s; Black Monday in 1987, when the Dow Jones Industrial Index lost 22.6 percent of its value in one day; the 1994 spike in interest rates that put rate-sensitive debt instruments into freefall; the emerging market crisis, Russian default and meltdown of Long-Term Capital Management in 1998; the bursting of the tech-stock bubble in 2000–2001; the accounting scandals of 2001–2002; and the worldwide financial crisis of 2007–2008.

Living through the 1970s was particularly formative, since so many challenges arose. It was virtually impossible to get an investment job during the seventies, meaning that in order to have experienced that decade, you had to have gotten your job before it started. How many of the people who started by the sixties were still working in the late nineties when the tech bubble rolled around? Not many. Most professional investors had joined the industry in the eighties or nineties and didn't know a market decline could exceed 5 percent, the greatest drop seen between 1982 and 1999.

///

SETH KLARMAN: *This fact may be one of the most shocking statements in this book. During this period, investors were lulled to sleep, anticipating double-digit annual returns while completely losing sight of the risks. Seventeen years ought to qualify as long term—it is roughly half of a career—yet a career built only during this period would hardly have withstood the test of time.*

\\\

If you read widely, you can learn from people whose ideas merit publishing. Some of the most important for me were Charley Ellis's great article "The Loser's Game" (*The Financial Analysts Journal*, July-August 1975), *A Short History of Financial Euphoria*, by John Kenneth Galbraith (New York:

Viking, 1990) and Nassim Nicholas Taleb's *Fooled by Randomness* (New York: Texere, 2001). Each did a great deal to shape my thinking.

PAUL JOHNSON: *This is an excellent book list. Fortunately, students can now add* The Most Important Thing *to it!*

Finally, I've been extremely fortunate to learn directly from some outstanding thinkers: John Kenneth Galbraith on human foibles; Warren Buffett on patience and contrarianism; Charlie Munger on the importance of reasonable expectations; Bruce Newberg on "probability and outcome"; Michael Milken on conscious risk bearing; and Ric Kayne on setting "traps" (underrated investment opportunities where you can make a lot but can't lose a lot). I've also benefited from my association with Peter Bernstein, Seth Klarman, Jack Bogle, Jacob Rothschild, Jeremy Grantham, Joel Greenblatt, Tony Pace, Orin Kramer, Jim Grant and Doug Kass.

The happy truth is that I was exposed to all of these elements and aware enough to combine them into the investment philosophy that has worked for my organizations—and thus for my clients—for many years. It's not the only right one—there are lots of ways to skin the cat—but it's right for us.

I hasten to point out that my philosophy wouldn't have meant much without skilled implementation on the part of my incredible Oaktree cofounders—Bruce Karsh, Sheldon Stone, Larry Keele, Richard Masson and Steve Kaplan—with whom I was fortunate to team up between 1983 and 1993. I'm convinced that no idea can be any better than the action taken on it, and that's especially true in the world of investing. The philosophy I share here wouldn't have attracted attention were it not for the accomplishments of these partners and the rest of my Oaktree colleagues.

HOWARD MARKS: *Through these annotations I want to recognize the wonderful people who contributed to the making of this book: Bridget Flannery-McCoy, Milenda Lee, Jennifer Jerome, Meredith Howard, and Noah Arlow of Columbia University Press, as well as my editorial consultant, Maggie Stuckey. Above all, I want to thank Myles Thompson for coming to me with the idea of doing a book with Columbia and guiding it to fruition. Finally, I want to add mention of my friend Peter Kaufman, who has contributed to my thinking by suggesting noninvestment parallels.*

THE MOST IMPORTANT THING

ILLUMINATED

1

The Most Important Thing Is . . .
Second-Level Thinking

The art of investment has one characteristic that is not generally appreciated. A creditable, if unspectacular, result can be achieved by the lay investor with a minimum of effort and capability; but to improve this easily attainable standard requires much application and more than a trace of wisdom.

BEN GRAHAM, *THE INTELLIGENT INVESTOR*

Everything should be made as simple as possible, but not simpler.

ALBERT EINSTEIN

It's not supposed to be easy. Anyone who finds it easy is stupid.

CHARLIE MUNGER

Few people have what it takes to be great investors. Some can be taught, but not everyone . . . and those who *can* be taught can't be taught everything. Valid approaches work some of the time but not all. And investing can't be reduced to an algorithm and turned over to a computer. Even the best investors don't get it right every time.

The reasons are simple. No rule always works. The environment isn't controllable, and circumstances rarely repeat exactly. Psychology plays a major role in markets, and because it's highly variable, cause-and-effect relationships aren't reliable. An investment approach may work for a while, but eventually the actions it calls for will change the environment, meaning a new approach is needed. And if others emulate an approach, that will blunt its effectiveness.

Investing, like economics, is more art than science. And that means it can get a little messy.

> One of the most important things to bear in mind today is that economics isn't an exact science. It may not even be much of a science at all, in the sense that in science, controlled experiments can be conducted, past results can be replicated with confidence, and cause-and-effect relationships can be depended on to hold.
>
> "WILL IT WORK?" MARCH 5, 2009

Because investing is at least as much art as it is science, it's never my goal—in this book or elsewhere—to suggest it can be routinized. In fact, one of the things I most want to emphasize is how essential it is that one's investment approach be intuitive and adaptive rather than be fixed and mechanistic.

~

At bottom, it's a matter of what you're trying to accomplish. Anyone can achieve average investment performance—just invest in an index fund that buys a little of everything. That will give you what is known as "market returns"—merely matching whatever the market does. But successful investors want more. They want to beat the market.

SETH KLARMAN: *Beating the market matters, but limiting risk matters just as much. Ultimately, investors have to ask themselves whether they are interested in relative or absolute returns. Losing 45 percent while the market drops 50 percent qualifies as market outperformance, but what a pyrrhic victory this would be for most of us.*

In my view, that's the definition of successful investing: doing better than the market and other investors.

CHRISTOPHER DAVIS: *The subtext here is that you must be patient and give yourself ample time—you're not looking for short-term windfalls but for long-term, steady returns.*

To accomplish that, you need either good luck or superior insight. Counting on luck isn't much of a plan, so you'd better concentrate on insight. In basketball they say, "You can't coach height," meaning all the coaching in the world won't make a player taller. It's almost as hard to teach insight. As with any other art form, some people just understand investing better than others. They have—or manage to acquire—that necessary "trace of wisdom" that Ben Graham so eloquently calls for.

Everyone wants to make money. All of economics is based on belief in the universality of the profit motive. So is capitalism; the profit motive makes people work harder and risk their capital. The pursuit of profit has produced much of the material progress the world has enjoyed.

But that universality also makes beating the market a difficult task. Millions of people are competing for each available dollar of investment gain. Who'll get it? The person who's a step ahead. In some pursuits, getting to the front of the pack means more schooling, more time in the gym or the library, better nutrition, more perspiration, greater stamina or better equipment. But in investing, where these things count for less, it calls for more perceptive thinking . . . at what I call the second level.

Would-be investors can take courses in finance and accounting, read widely and, if they are fortunate, receive mentoring from someone with a deep understanding of the investment process. But only a few of them will achieve the superior insight, intuition, sense of value and awareness of psychology that are required for consistently above-average results. Doing so requires second-level thinking.

~

Remember, your goal in investing isn't to earn average returns; you want to do better than average. Thus, your thinking has to be better than that of others—both more powerful and at a higher level. Since other investors may be smart, well-informed and highly computerized, you must find an edge they don't have. You must think of something they haven't thought of, see things they miss or bring insight they don't possess. You have to react differently and behave differently. In short, being right may be a necessary condition for investment success, but it won't be sufficient. You must be more right than others . . . which by definition means your thinking has to be different.

PAUL JOHNSON: *Marks's comments in this paragraph are excellent. He successfully articulates the critical importance of second-level thinking to investment success. The short discussion that follows offers three excellent examples of the difference between first- and second-level thinking.*

What is second-level thinking?

- First-level thinking says, "It's a good company; let's buy the stock." Second-level thinking says, "It's a good company, but everyone thinks it's a great company, and it's not. So the stock's overrated and overpriced; let's sell."

JOEL GREENBLATT: *I hear first-level thinking from individual investors all the time. They read the headlines or watch CNBC and then adopt conventional first-level investment opinions.*

- First-level thinking says, "The outlook calls for low growth and rising inflation. Let's dump our stocks." Second-level thinking says, "The outlook stinks, but everyone else is selling in panic. Buy!"
- First-level thinking says, "I think the company's earnings will fall; sell." Second-level thinking says, "I think the company's earnings will fall less than people expect, and the pleasant surprise will lift the stock; buy."

First-level thinking is simplistic and superficial, and just about everyone can do it (a bad sign for anything involving an attempt at superiority). All the first-level thinker needs is an opinion about the future, as in "The outlook for the company is favorable, meaning the stock will go up."

Second-level thinking is deep, complex and convoluted. The second-level thinker takes a great many things into account:

- What is the range of likely future outcomes?
- Which outcome do I think will occur?

- What's the probability I'm right?
- What does the consensus think?
- How does my expectation differ from the consensus?
- How does the current price for the asset comport with the consensus view of the future, and with mine?
- Is the consensus psychology that's incorporated in the price too bullish or bearish?
- What will happen to the asset's price if the consensus turns out to be right, and what if I'm right?

CHRISTOPHER DAVIS: *This is a good reminder of questions you should always ask yourself when evaluating new investments. It's easy to forget this in the excitement of a new opportunity.*

The difference in workload between first-level and second-level thinking is clearly massive, and the number of people capable of the latter is tiny compared to the number capable of the former.

First-level thinkers look for simple formulas and easy answers. Second-level thinkers know that success in investing is the antithesis of simple. That's not to say you won't run into plenty of people who try their darnedest to make it sound simple. Some of them I might characterize as "mercenaries." Brokerage firms want you to think everyone's capable of investing—at $10 per trade. Mutual fund companies don't want you to think you can do it; they want you to think *they* can do it. In that case, you'll put your money into actively managed funds and pay the associated high fees.

Others who simplify are what I think of as "proselytizers." Some are academics who teach investing. Others are well-intentioned practitioners who overestimate the extent to which they're in control; I think most of them fail to tote up their records, or they overlook their bad years or attribute losses to bad luck. Finally, there are those who simply fail to understand the complexity of the subject. A guest commentator on my drive-time radio station says, "If you have had good experience with a product, buy the stock." There's so much more than that to being a successful investor.

First-level thinkers think the same way other first-level thinkers do about the same things, and they generally reach the same conclusions. By definition, this can't be the route to superior results. All investors can't beat the market since, collectively, they are the market.

Before trying to compete in the zero-sum world of investing, you must ask yourself whether you have good reason to expect to be in the top half. To outperform the average investor, you have to be able to outthink the consensus. Are you capable of doing so? What makes you think so?

CHRISTOPHER DAVIS: *You can also invert this—in addition to asking yourself how and why you should succeed, ask yourself why others fail. Is there a problem with their time horizons? Are their incentive systems flawed or inappropriate?*

The problem is that extraordinary performance comes only from correct nonconsensus forecasts, but nonconsensus forecasts are hard to make, hard to make correctly and hard to act on. Over the years, many people have told me that the matrix shown below had an impact on them:

PAUL JOHNSON: *The concepts in this section are critically important if an investor is going to have the correct viewpoint to deliver superior investment performance. The wisdom espoused in this section alone is worth the price of the book.*

You can't do the same things others do and expect to outperform. . . . Unconventionality shouldn't be a goal in itself, but rather a way of thinking. In order to distinguish yourself from others, it helps to have ideas that are different and to process those ideas differently. I conceptualize the situation as a simple 2-by-2 matrix:

	Conventional Behavior	Unconventional Behavior
Favorable Outcomes	Average good results	Above-average results
Unfavorable Outcomes	Average bad results	Below-average results

Of course it's not that easy and clear-cut, but I think that's the general situation. If your behavior is conventional, you're likely to get conventional results—either good or bad. Only if your behavior is unconventional is your performance likely to be unconventional, and only if your judgments are superior is your performance likely to be above average.

"DARE TO BE GREAT," SEPTEMBER 7, 2006

The upshot is simple: to achieve superior investment results, you have to hold nonconsensus views regarding value, and they have to be accurate. That's not easy.

The attractiveness of buying something for less than it's worth makes eminent sense. So how is one to find bargains in efficient markets? You must bring exceptional analytical ability, insight or foresight. But because it's exceptional, few people have it.

"RETURNS AND HOW THEY GET THAT WAY," NOVEMBER 11, 2002

For your performance to diverge from the norm, your expectations—and thus your portfolio—have to diverge from the norm, and you have to be more right than the consensus. Different and better: that's a pretty good description of second-level thinking.

Those who consider the investment process simple generally aren't aware of the need for—or even the existence of—second-level thinking. Thus, many people are misled into believing that everyone can be a successful investor. Not everyone can. But the good news is that the prevalence of first-level thinkers increases the returns available to second-level thinkers. To consistently achieve superior investment returns, you must be one of them.

//

JOEL GREENBLATT: *The idea is that agreeing with the broad consensus, while a very comfortable place for most people to be, is not generally where above-average profits are found.*

\\

2

The Most Important Thing Is . . . Understanding Market Efficiency (and Its Limitations)

The 1960s saw the emergence of a new theory of finance and investing, a body of thought known as the "Chicago School" because of its origins at the University of Chicago's Graduate School of Business. As a student there in 1967–1969, I found myself at ground zero for this new theory. It greatly informed and influenced my thinking.

The theory included concepts that went on to become important elements in investment dialogue: risk aversion, volatility as the definition of risk, risk-adjusted returns, systematic and nonsystematic risk, alpha, beta, the random walk hypothesis and the efficient market hypothesis. (All of these are addressed in the pages that follow.) In the years since it was first proposed, that last concept has proved to be particularly influential in the field of investing, so significant that it deserves its own chapter.

The efficient market hypothesis states that

- There are many participants in the markets, and they share roughly equal access to all relevant information. They are intelligent, objective, highly motivated and hardworking. Their analytical models are widely known and employed.

- Because of the collective efforts of these participants, information is reflected fully and immediately in the market price of each asset. And because market participants will move instantly to buy any asset that's too cheap or sell one that's too dear, assets are priced fairly in the absolute and relative to each other.
- Thus, market prices represent accurate estimates of assets' intrinsic value, and no participant can consistently identify and profit from instances when they are wrong.
- Assets therefore sell at prices from which they can be expected to deliver risk-adjusted returns that are "fair" relative to other assets. Riskier assets must offer higher returns in order to attract buyers. The market will set prices so that appears to be the case, but it won't provide a "free lunch." That is, there will be no incremental return that is not related to (and compensatory for) incremental risk.

That's a more or less official summary of the highlights. Now my take. When I speak of this theory, I also use the word *efficient*, but I mean it in the sense of "speedy, quick to incorporate information," not "right."

PAUL JOHNSON: *Marks's definition of "efficient" is functional and works well with students.*

I agree that because investors work hard to evaluate every new piece of information, asset prices immediately reflect the consensus view of the information's significance. I do not, however, believe the consensus view is necessarily correct. In January 2000, Yahoo sold at $237. In April 2001 it was at $11. Anyone who argues that the market was right both times has his or her head in the clouds; it has to have been wrong on at least one of those occasions. But that doesn't mean many investors were able to detect and act on the market's error.

If prices in efficient markets already reflect the consensus, then sharing the consensus view will make you likely to earn just an average return. To beat the market you must hold an idiosyncratic, or nonconsensus, view.

PAUL JOHNSON: *Here, Marks successfully links market efficiency with second-level thinking. This statement is a very important contribution to investment literature because few commentators have attempted to link academic work on market theory with a pragmatic view of how to actively manage assets.*

The bottom line for me is that, although the more efficient markets often misvalue assets, it's not easy for any one person—working with the same information as everyone else and subject to the same psychological influences—to consistently hold views that are different from the consensus *and* closer to being correct.

SETH KLARMAN: *Psychological influences are a dominating factor governing investor behavior. They matter as much as—and at times more than—underlying value in determining securities prices.*

CHRISTOPHER DAVIS: *It is also critical to spend time trying to fully understand the incentives at work in any given situation. Flawed incentives can often explain irrational, destructive, or counterintuitive behaviors or outcomes.*

That's what makes the mainstream markets awfully hard to beat—even if they aren't always right.

"WHAT'S IT ALL ABOUT, ALPHA?" JULY 11, 2001

The most important upshot from the efficient market hypothesis is its conclusion that "you can't beat the market." Not only was this conclusion founded logically on the Chicago view of the market, but it was buttressed by studies of the performance of mutual funds. Very few of those funds have distinguished themselves through their results.

What about the five-star funds? you might ask. Read the small print: mutual funds are rated relative to each other. The ratings don't say anything about their having beaten an objective standard such as a market index.

Okay then, what about the celebrated investors we hear so much about? First, one or two good years prove nothing; chance alone can produce just about any result. Second, statisticians insist nothing can be proved with statistical significance until you have enough years of data; I remember a figure of sixty-four years, and almost no one manages money that long. Finally, the emergence of one or two great investors doesn't disprove the theory. The fact that the Warren Buffetts of this world attract as much attention as they do is an indication that consistent outperformers are exceptional.

One of the greatest ramifications of the Chicago theory has been the development of passive investment vehicles known as *index funds*. If most active portfolio managers making "active bets" on which securities to overweight and underweight can't beat the market, why pay the price—in the form of transaction costs and management fees—entailed in trying? With that question in mind, investors have put growing amounts in funds that simply invest a market-determined amount in each stock or bond in a market index. In this way, investors enjoy market returns at a fee of just a few hundredths of a percent per year.

Everything moves in cycles, as I'll discuss later, and that includes "accepted wisdom." So the efficient market hypothesis got off to a fast start in the 1960s and developed a lot of adherents. Objections have been raised since then, and the general view of its applicability rises and falls.

~

I have my own reservations about the theory, and the biggest one has to do with the way it links return and risk.

According to investment theory, people are risk-averse by nature, meaning that in general they'd rather bear less risk than more. For them to make riskier investments, they have to be induced through the promise of higher returns. Thus, markets will adjust the prices of investments so that, based on the known facts and common perceptions, the riskier ones will appear to promise higher returns.

Because theory says in an efficient market there's no such thing as investing skill (commonly referred to today as *alpha*) that would enable someone to beat the market, all the difference in return between one investment and another—or between one person's portfolio and another's—is attributable to differences in risk. In fact, if you show an adherent of the efficient market hypothesis an investment record that appears to be superior, as I have, the answer is likely to be, "The higher return is explained by hidden risk." (The fallback position is to say, "You don't have enough years of data.")

Once in a while we experience periods when everything goes well and riskier investments deliver the higher returns they seem to promise. Those halcyon periods lull people into believing that to get higher returns, all they have to do is make riskier investments. But they ignore something that is easily forgotten in good times: this can't be true, because if riskier investments could be counted on to produce higher returns, they wouldn't be riskier.

Every once in a while, then, people learn an essential lesson. They realize that nothing—and certainly not the indiscriminate acceptance of risk—carries the promise of a free lunch, and they're reminded of the limitations of investment theory.

~

That's the theory and its implications. The key question is whether it's right: Is the market unbeatable? Are the people who try wasting their time? Are the clients who pay fees to investment managers wasting their money? As with most other things in my world, the answers aren't simple . . . and they're certainly not yes or no.

I don't believe the notion of market efficiency deserves to be dismissed out of hand. In principle, it's fair to conclude that if thousands of rational and numerate people gather information about an asset and evaluate it diligently and objectively, the asset's price shouldn't stray far from its intrinsic value. Mispricings shouldn't be regularly extant, meaning it should be hard to beat the market.

In fact, some asset classes are quite efficient. In most of these:

- the asset class is widely known and has a broad following;
- the class is socially acceptable, not controversial or taboo;
- the merits of the class are clear and comprehensible, at least on the surface; and
- information about the class and its components is distributed widely and evenly.

SETH KLARMAN: *Most of these characteristics are not permanent. Something broadly accepted can become controversial or even taboo. Information can become more or less available. Thus, an asset class deemed close to efficient at one point may become quite inefficient at another. European sovereign debt is a current example of this.*

If these conditions are met, there's no reason why the asset class should systematically be overlooked, misunderstood or underrated.

///

PAUL JOHNSON: *Inverting these conditions yields a test of market inefficiency. For instance, in the first case, if an asset is not widely known and broadly followed, it might be inefficiently priced; in the second case, if an asset is controversial, taboo, or socially unacceptable, it might be inefficiently priced; and so on for each of the other two cases.*

\\

Take foreign exchange, for example. What are the things that determine the movements of one currency versus another? Future growth rates and inflation rates. Is it possible for any one person to systematically know much more about these things than everyone else? Probably not. And if not, then no one should be able to regularly achieve above-average risk-adjusted returns through currency trading.

What about the major stock markets, such as the New York Stock Exchange? Here millions of people are prospecting, driven by the desire for profit. They're all similarly informed; in fact, it's one of the goals of our market regulation that everyone should gain access to the same company information at the same time. With millions of people doing similar analysis on the basis of similar information, how often will stocks become mispriced, and how regularly can any one person detect those mispricings?

Answer: Not often, and not dependably. But that is the essence of second-level thinking.

Second-level thinkers know that, to achieve superior results, they have to have an edge in either information or analysis, or both. They are on the alert for instances of misperception. My son Andrew is a budding investor, and he comes up with lots of appealing investment ideas based on today's facts and the outlook for tomorrow. But he's been well trained. His first test is always the same: "And who doesn't know that?"

∽

In the vocabulary of the theory, second-level thinkers depend on *inefficiency*. The term *inefficiency* came into widespread use over the last forty years as the counterpoint to the belief that investors can't beat the market. To me, describing a market as inefficient is a high-flown way of saying the market is prone to mistakes that can be taken advantage of.

Where might errors come from? Let's consider the assumptions that underlie the theory of efficient markets:

- There are many investors hard at work.
- They are intelligent, diligent, objective, motivated and well equipped.
- They all have access to the available information, and their access is roughly equal.
- They're all open to buying, selling or shorting (i.e., betting against) every asset.

For those reasons, theory says that all the available information will be smoothly and efficiently synthesized into prices and acted on whenever price/value discrepancies arise, so as to drive out those discrepancies.

But it's impossible to argue that market prices are always right. In fact, if you look at the four assumptions just listed, one stands out as particularly tenuous: objectivity. Human beings are not clinical computing machines. Rather, most people are driven by greed, fear, envy and other emotions that render objectivity impossible and open the door for significant mistakes.

Likewise, what about the fourth assumption? Whereas investors are supposed to be open to any asset—and to both owning it and being short—the truth is very different. Most professionals are assigned to particular market niches, as in "I work in the equity department" or "I'm a bond manager."

SETH KLARMAN: *Silos are a double-edged sword. A narrow focus leads to potentially superior knowledge. But concentration of effort within rigid boundaries leaves a strong possibility of mispricings outside those borders. Also, if others' silos are similar to your own, competitive forces will likely drive down returns in spite of superior knowledge within such silos.*

And the percentage of investors who ever sell short is truly tiny. Who, then, makes and implements the decisions that would drive out relative mispricings between asset classes?

A market characterized by mistakes and mispricings can be beaten by people with rare insight. Thus, the existence of inefficiencies gives rise to the possibility of outperformance and is a necessary condition for it. It does not, however, guarantee it.

To me, an inefficient market is one that is marked by at least one (and probably, as a result, by all) of the following characteristics:

- Market prices are often wrong. Because access to information and the analysis thereof are highly imperfect, market prices are often far above or far below intrinsic values.
- The risk-adjusted return on one asset class can be far out of line with those of other asset classes. Because assets are often valued at other-than-fair prices, an asset class can deliver a risk-adjusted return that is significantly too high (a free lunch) or too low relative to other asset classes.
- Some investors can consistently outperform others. Because of the existence of (a) significant misvaluations and (b) differences among participants in terms of skill, insight and information access, it is possible for misvaluations to be identified and profited from with regularity.

This last point is very important in terms of what it does and does not mean. Inefficient markets do not necessarily give their participants generous returns. Rather, it's my view that they provide the raw material—mispricings—that can allow some people to win *and others to lose* on the basis of differential skill. If prices can be very wrong, that means it's possible to find bargains *or overpay.* For every person who gets a good buy in an inefficient market, someone else sells too cheap. One of the great sayings about poker is that "in every game there's a fish. If you've played for 45 minutes and haven't figured out who the fish is, then it's you." The same is certainly true of inefficient market investing.

"WHAT'S IT ALL ABOUT, ALPHA?" JULY 11, 2001

∼

In the great debate over efficiency versus inefficiency, I have concluded that no market is completely one or the other. It's just a matter of degree. I wholeheartedly appreciate the opportunities that inefficiency can provide, but I also respect the concept of market efficiency, and I believe strongly that mainstream securities markets can be so efficient that it's largely a waste of time to work at finding winners there.

PAUL JOHNSON: *This idea is extremely important because business schools tend to push the debate to one extreme or the other. Many of the academics want to argue for full market efficiency, which forces the practitioners to argue the opposite just to keep a balanced discussion. Marks offers a significantly superior way to manage the topic. A corollary that follows from Marks's observation is that investors should look for markets or assets that are not fully efficiently priced rather than chase after the false god of completely inefficient markets.*

In the end, I've come to an interesting resolution: Efficiency is not so universal that we should give up on superior performance. At the same time, efficiency is what lawyers call a "rebuttable presumption"—something that should be presumed to be true until someone proves otherwise. Therefore, we should assume that efficiency will impede our achievement unless we have good reason to believe it won't in the present case.

Respect for efficiency says that before we embark on a course of action, we should ask some questions: have mistakes and mispricings been driven out through investors' concerted efforts, or do they still exist, and why?

Think of it this way:

- Why should a bargain exist despite the presence of thousands of investors who stand ready and willing to bid up the price of anything that's too cheap?
- If the return appears so generous in proportion to the risk, might you be overlooking some hidden risk?
- Why would the seller of the asset be willing to part with it at a price from which it will give you an excessive return?
- Do you really know more about the asset than the seller does?
- If it's such a great proposition, why hasn't someone else snapped it up?

Something else to keep in mind: just because efficiencies exist today doesn't mean they'll remain forever.

Bottom line: Inefficiency is a necessary condition for superior investing. Attempting to outperform in a perfectly efficient market is like flipping a fair coin: the best you can hope for is fifty-fifty. For investors to get an edge, there have to be inefficiencies in the underlying process—imperfections, mispricings—to take advantage of.

But let's say there are. That alone is not a sufficient condition for outperformance. All that means is that prices aren't always fair and mistakes are occurring: some assets are priced too low and some too high. You still have to be more insightful than others in order to regularly buy more of the former than the latter. Many of the best bargains at any point in time are found among the things other investors can't or won't do.

JOEL GREENBLATT: *This is very important and helps explain why most professionals have a hard time beating the market. Investments that are out of favor, that don't look so attractive in the near term, are avoided by most professionals, who feel they need to add performance right now.*

Let others believe markets can never be beat. Abstention on the part of those who won't venture in creates opportunities for those who will.

∾

Is investment theory, with its notion of market efficiency, the equivalent of a physical law that is universally true? Or is it an irrelevant ivory-tower notion to be disregarded? In the end, it's a question of balance, and balance comes from applying informed common sense. The key turning point in my investment management career came when I concluded that because the notion of market efficiency has relevance, I should limit my efforts to relatively inefficient markets where hard work and skill would pay off best.

JOEL GREENBLATT: *Of course, some markets are more inefficient because they are less closely followed in general, but portions of widely followed markets, like common stocks, can also be inefficient. Stocks with smaller capitalization or stocks of companies going through extraordinary events come to mind.*

Theory informed that decision and prevented me from wasting my time in the mainstream markets, but it took an understanding of the limits of the theory to keep me from completely accepting the arguments against active management.

In short, I think theory should inform our decisions but not dominate them. If we entirely ignore theory, we can make big mistakes. We can fool ourselves into thinking it's possible to know more than everyone else and to regularly beat heavily populated markets. We can buy securities for their returns but ignore their risk. We can buy fifty correlated securities and mistakenly think we've diversified. . . .

But swallowing theory whole can make us give up on finding bargains, turn the process over to a computer and miss out on the contribution skillful individuals can make. The image here is of the efficient-market-believing finance professor who takes a walk with a student.

"Isn't that a $10 bill lying on the ground?" asks the student.

"No, it can't be a $10 bill," answers the professor. "If it were, someone would have picked it up by now."

The professor walks away, and the student picks it up and has a beer.

"WHAT'S IT ALL ABOUT, ALPHA?" JULY 11, 2001

3

The Most Important Thing Is . . . Value

For investing to be reliably successful, an accurate estimate of intrinsic value is the indispensable starting
point. Without it, any hope for consistent success as an
investor is just that: hope.

JOEL GREENBLATT: *Warren Buffett says that the best investment
course would teach just two things well: How to value an investment and how to think about market price movements. Step one
starts right here.*

The oldest rule in investing is also the simplest: "Buy low; sell high." Seems
blindingly obvious: Who would want to do anything else? But what does
that rule actually mean? Again, obvious—on the surface: it means that you
should buy something at a low price and sell it at a high price. But what, in
turn, does *that* mean? What's high, and what's low?

On a superficial level, you can take it to mean that the goal is to buy
something for less than you sell it for. But since your sale will take place
well down the road, that's not much help in figuring out the proper price at
which to buy today. There has to be some objective standard for "high" and
"low," and most usefully that standard is the asset's intrinsic value. Now the
meaning of the saying becomes clear: buy at a price below intrinsic value,
and sell at a higher price. Of course, to do that, you'd better have a good

idea what intrinsic value is. For me, an accurate estimate of value is the indispensable starting point.

PAUL JOHNSON: This is the first building block of value investing.

~

To simplify (or oversimplify), all approaches to investing in company securities can be divided into two basic types: those based on analysis of the company's attributes, known as "fundamentals," and those based on study of the price behavior of the securities themselves. In other words, an investor has two basic choices: gauge the security's underlying intrinsic value and buy or sell when the price diverges from it, or base decisions purely on expectations regarding future price movements.

I'll turn to the latter first, since I don't believe in it and should be able to dispose of it rather promptly. *Technical analysis*, or the study of past stock price behavior, has been practiced ever since I joined the industry (and well before that), but it's been in decline. Today observations about historic price patterns may be used to supplement fundamental analysis, but we hear far less than we did in the past about people basing decisions primarily on what price movements tell them.

Part of the decline of technical analysis can be attributed to the *random walk hypothesis*, a component of the Chicago theory developed in the early 1960s, primarily by Professor Eugene Fama. The random walk hypothesis says a stock's past price movements are of absolutely no help in predicting future movements. In other words, it's a random process, like tossing a coin. We all know that even if a coin has come up heads ten times in a row, the probability of heads on the next throw is still fifty-fifty. Likewise, the hypothesis says, the fact that a stock's price has risen for the last ten days tells you nothing about what it will do tomorrow.

Another form of relying on past stock price movements to tell you something is so-called momentum investing. It, too, exists in contravention of the random walk hypothesis. I'm unlikely to do it justice. But as I see it, investors who practice this approach operate under the assumption that they can tell when something that has been rising will continue to rise.

Momentum investing might enable you to participate in a bull market that continues upward, but I see a lot of drawbacks. One is based on economist Herb Stein's wry observation that "if something cannot go on forever, it will stop." What happens to momentum investors then? How will this approach help them sell in time to avoid a decline? And what will it have them do in falling markets?

It seems clear that momentum investing isn't a cerebral approach to investing. The greatest example came in 1998–1999, with the rise of people called day traders. Most were nonprofessional investors drawn from other walks of life by the hope for easy money in the tech-media-telecom stock boom. They rarely held positions overnight, since doing so would require them to pay for them. Several times a day, they would try to guess whether a stock they'd been watching would rise or fall in the next few hours.

I've never understood how people reach conclusions like these. I liken it to trying to guess whether the next person to come around the corner will be male or female. The way I see it, day traders considered themselves successful if they bought a stock at $10 and sold at $11, bought it back the next week at $24 and sold at $25, and bought it a week later at $39 and sold at $40. If you can't see the flaw in this—that the trader made $3 in a stock that appreciated by $30—you probably shouldn't read the rest of this book.

Moving away from momentum investors and their Ouija boards, along with all other forms of investing that eschew intelligent analysis, we are left with two approaches, both driven by fundamentals: *value investing* and *growth investing*. In a nutshell, value investors aim to come up with a security's current intrinsic value and buy when the price is lower, and growth investors try to find securities whose value will increase rapidly in the future.

> To value investors, an asset isn't an ephemeral concept you invest in because you think it's attractive (or think others will find it attractive). It's a tangible object that should have an intrinsic value capable of being ascertained, and if it can be bought below its intrinsic value, you might consider doing so. Thus, intelligent investing has to be built on estimates of intrinsic value. Those estimates must be derived rigorously, based on all of the available information.
>
> "THE MOST IMPORTANT THING," JULY 1, 2003

///

JOEL GREENBLATT: *This estimate of value includes an estimate for future growth in earnings or cash flow.*

\\

What is it that makes a security—or the underlying company—valuable? There are lots of candidates: financial resources, management, factories, retail outlets, patents, human resources, brand names, growth potential and, most of all, the ability to generate earnings and cash flow. In fact, most analytical approaches would say that all those other characteristics—financial resources, management, factories, retail outlets, patents, human resources, brand names and growth potential—are valuable precisely because they can translate eventually into earnings and cash flow.

The emphasis in value investing is on tangible factors like hard assets and cash flows. Intangibles like talent, popular fashions and long-term growth potential are given less weight. Certain strains of value investing focus exclusively on hard assets. There's even something called "net-net investing," in which people buy when the total market value of a company's stock is less than the amount by which the company's current assets—such as cash, receivables and inventories—exceed its total liabilities. In this case, in theory, you could buy all the stock, liquidate the current assets, pay off the debts, and end up with the business and some cash. Pocket cash equal to your cost, and with more left over you'll have paid "less than nothing" for the business.

The quest in value investing is for cheapness. Value investors typically look at financial metrics such as earnings, cash flow, dividends, hard assets and enterprise value and emphasize buying cheap on these bases. The primary goal of value investors, then, is to quantify the company's current value and buy its securities when they can do so cheaply.

Growth investing lies somewhere between the dull plodding of value investing and the adrenaline charge of momentum investing. Its goal is to identify companies with bright futures. That means by definition that there's less emphasis on the company's current attributes and more on its potential.

The difference between the two principal schools of investing can be boiled down to this:

- *Value investors* buy stocks (even those whose intrinsic value may show little growth in the future) out of conviction that the current value is high relative to the current price.

- *Growth investors* buy stocks (even those whose current value is low relative to their current price) because they believe the value will grow fast enough in the future to produce substantial appreciation.

Thus, it seems to me, the choice isn't really between value and growth, but between value today and value tomorrow. Growth investing represents a bet on company performance that may or may not materialize in the future, while value investing is based primarily on analysis of a company's current worth.

"THE HAPPY MEDIUM," JULY 21, 2004

JOEL GREENBLATT: *One of Buffett's major contributions has been to extend the idea of value beyond the simply "cheap." Buffett looks for "good" businesses that are available at an attractive price. The concept of growth is incorporated into the calculation of value.*

It would be convenient to say that adherence to value investing permits investors to *avoid* conjecture about the future and that growth investing *consists only* of conjecture about the future, but that would be a considerable exaggeration. After all, establishing the current value of a business requires an opinion regarding its future, and that in turn must take into account the likely macro-economic environment, competitive developments and technological advances. Even a promising net-net investment can be doomed if the company's assets are squandered on money-losing operations or unwise acquisitions.

There's no bright-line distinction between value and growth; both require us to deal with the future. Value investors think about the company's potential for growth, and the "growth at a reasonable price" school pays explicit homage to value. It's all a matter of degree. However, I think it can fairly be said that growth investing is about the future, whereas value investing emphasizes current-day considerations but can't escape dealing with the future.

∾

For an extreme example of growth investing, let me take you back to the days of the Nifty Fifty, a fad that epitomized the contrast with value investing and demonstrates how far a growth mania can go.

In 1968 I had my first job in the investment management industry, as a summer employee in the Investment Research Department of First National City Bank (now Citibank). The bank followed an approach known as "Nifty Fifty investing." Its goal was to identify the companies with the brightest outlook for earnings growth over the long term. In addition to growth rate, the bank's investment managers stressed "quality," by which they meant a high probability that the growth expectations would be realized. It was official dictum that if a company was growing fast enough and of sufficient quality, the price paid for the stock didn't matter. If a stock is expensive based on today's metrics, give it a few years and it'll grow into its price.

Then, as now, growth stock portfolios were heavily weighted toward drugs, technology and consumer products. The bank's portfolios included highly respected names such as IBM, Xerox, Kodak, Polaroid, Merck, Eli Lilly, Avon, Coca-Cola, Philip Morris, Hewlett-Packard, Motorola, Texas Instruments and Perkin-Elmer—America's great companies, all with bright outlooks for growth. Since nothing could go wrong at these companies, there was no hesitance to pay up for their stocks.

Fast-forward a couple of decades, and what do you see in that list of companies? Some, such as Kodak and Polaroid, have seen their basic businesses decimated by unforeseen changes in technology. Others, such as IBM and Xerox, became slow-moving prey on which new competitors feasted. All told, First National City's list of America's best companies has been visited by deterioration and even bankruptcy in the forty-two years since I started. So much for the long-term persistence of growth—and for the ability to predict it accurately.

CHRISTOPHER DAVIS: *Interestingly, this portfolio—if purchased in 1968 and held until today—eventually beat the market, but it took decades to get out of the hole and succeeded only because of the tremendous outperformance of Philip Morris. Although the principle is correct (that overpaying destroys returns) this example is also a reminder of the difference between stocks and bonds. Because stocks represent ownership interests in businesses that have essentially unlimited duration; if you are right about the business, time can reduce the cost of overpaying. In some rare cases (like Philip Morris) it is possible to benefit from the "miracle" of compounding at double-digit rates for more than forty years. As far as I know, this opportunity has never been available in fixed-income investment.*

Compared to value investing, growth investing centers around trying for big winners. If big winners weren't in the offing, why put up with the uncertainty entailed in guessing at the future? There's no question about it: it's harder to see the future than the present. Thus, the batting average for growth investors should be lower, but the payoff for doing it well might be higher. The return for correctly predicting which companies will come up with the best new drug, most powerful computer or best-selling movies should be substantial.

In general, the upside potential for being right about growth is more dramatic, and the upside potential for being right about value is more consistent. Value is my approach. In my book, consistency trumps drama.

~

If value investing has the potential to consistently produce favorable results, does that mean it's easy? No.

For one thing, it depends on an accurate estimate of value. Without that, any hope for consistent success as an investor is just that: hope. Without accurate estimates, you'll be as likely to overpay as to underpay. And if you overpay, it takes a surprising improvement in value, a strong market or an even less discriminating buyer (what we used to call a "greater fool") to bail you out.

There's more. If you've settled on the value approach to investing and come up with an intrinsic value for a security or asset, the next important thing is to hold it firmly. That's because in the world of investing, being correct about something isn't at all synonymous with being proved correct right away.

It's hard to consistently do the right thing as an investor. But it's impossible to consistently do the right thing at the right time. The most we value investors can hope for is to be right about an asset's value and buy when it's available for less.

SETH KLARMAN: *Ideally, considerably less. The bigger the discount, the bigger your margin of safety. Too small a discount and the limited margin of safety provides no real protection at all.*

But doing so today certainly doesn't mean you're going to start making money tomorrow.

JOEL GREENBLATT: *I always tell my students, "If you do a good job valuing a stock, I guarantee that the market will agree with you." I just don't tell them when. It could be weeks or years. Graham said that the market is a "weighing machine" over the long term, even if it is often emotional over the short term. In my experience with the U.S. stock markets, two or three years is generally enough time for the market to get it "right." If you read the newspaper every day, this is often a tougher wait than it sounds.*

A firmly held view on value can help you cope with this disconnect.

Let's say you figure out that something's worth 80 and have a chance to buy it for 60. Chances to buy well below actual value don't come along every day, and you should welcome them. Warren Buffett describes them as "buying dollars for fifty cents." So you buy it and you feel you've done a good thing.

But don't expect immediate success. In fact, you'll often find that you've bought in the midst of a decline that continues. Pretty soon you'll be looking at losses. And as one of the greatest investment adages reminds us, "Being too far ahead of your time is indistinguishable from being wrong." So now that security worth 80 is priced at 50 instead of 60. What do you do?

JOEL GREENBLATT: *Unless you buy at the exact bottom tick (which is next to impossible), you will be down at some point after you make every investment.*

HOWARD MARKS: *My attempts to provide valuable annotations will concentrate on four important themes that run through the book; you'll see reference to them in many places. The first is something most investors don't think about enough: fear of looking wrong. Like participants in any field requiring the application of skill under challenging circumstances, superior investors' batting averages will be well below 1.000 and marked by errors and slumps. Judgments that prove correct don't necessarily do so promptly, so even the best investors look wrong a lot of the time. If you're not okay with that, try another field.*

We learn in Microeconomics 101 that the demand curve slopes downward to the right; as the price of something goes up, the quantity demanded goes down. In other words, people want less of something at higher prices and more of it at lower prices. Makes sense; that's why stores do more business when goods go on sale.

It works that way in most places, but far from always, it seems, in the world of investing. There, many people tend to fall further in love with the thing they've bought as its price rises, since they feel validated, and they like it less as the price falls, when they begin to doubt their decision to buy.

This makes it very difficult to hold, and to buy more at lower prices (which investors call "averaging down"), especially if the decline proves to be extensive. If you liked it at 60, you should like it more at 50 . . . and much more at 40 and 30.

SETH KLARMAN: *In some cases, value can be circular. Imagine a closed-end fund trading at a discount. If the underlying shares fall by 50 percent and the fund falls by the same percentage, it would superficially be no better a bargain at the reduced price. A proper analysis would involve an analysis of the underlying shareholdings to determine whether they were overvalued or undervalued in their own right.*

But it's not that easy. No one's comfortable with losses, and eventually any human will wonder, "Maybe it's not me who's right. Maybe it's the market." The danger is maximized when they start to think, "It's down so much, I'd better get out before it goes to zero." That's the kind of thinking that makes bottoms . . . and causes people to sell there.

Investors with no knowledge of (or concern for) profits, dividends, valuation or the conduct of business simply cannot possess the resolve needed to do the right thing at the right time. With everyone around them buying and making money, they can't know when a stock is too high and therefore resist joining in. And with a market in freefall, they can't possibly have the confidence needed to hold or buy at severely reduced prices.

"IRRATIONAL EXUBERANCE," MAY 1, 2000

An accurate opinion on valuation, loosely held, will be of limited help. An incorrect opinion on valuation, strongly held, is far worse. This one statement shows how hard it is to get it all right.

~

Give most investors—and certainly most amateur investors—a dose of truth serum, and then ask this question, "What's your approach to investing?" The inevitable answer: "I look for things that will go up." But the serious pursuit of profit has to be based on something more tangible. In my view, the best candidate for that something tangible is fundamentally derived intrinsic value. An accurate estimate of intrinsic value is the essential foundation for steady, unemotional and potentially profitable investing.

Value investors score their biggest gains when they buy an underpriced asset, average down unfailingly and have their analysis proved out. Thus, there are two essential ingredients for profit in a declining market: you have to have a view on intrinsic value, and you have to hold that view strongly enough to be able to hang in and buy even as price declines suggest that you're wrong. Oh yes, there's a third: you have to be right.

4

The Most Important Thing Is . . . The Relationship Between Price and Value

---

Investment success doesn't come from "buying good things," but rather from "buying things well."

Let's say you've become convinced of the efficacy of value investing and you're able to come up with an estimate of intrinsic value for a stock or other asset. Let's even say your estimate is right. You're not done. In order to know what action to take, you have to look at the asset's price relative to its value. Establishing a healthy relationship between fundamentals—value—and price is at the core of successful investing.

For a value investor, price has to be the starting point. It has been demonstrated time and time again that no asset is so good that it can't become a bad investment if bought at too high a price. And there are few assets so bad that they can't be a good investment when bought cheap enough.

//

CHRISTOPHER DAVIS: *However, investors should be wary of the risk of obsolescence, which can turn a cheap stock into a value trap.*

\\\

When people say flatly, "we only buy A" or "A is a superior asset class," that sounds a lot like "we'd buy A at any price . . . and we'd buy it before B, C or D at any price." That just has to be a mistake. No asset class or investment has the birthright of a high return. It's only attractive if it's priced right.

Hopefully, if I offered to sell you my car, you'd ask the price before saying yes or no. Deciding on an investment without carefully considering the fairness of its price is just as silly. But when people decide without disciplined consideration of valuation that they want to own something, as they did with tech stocks in the late 1990s—or that they simply won't own something, as they did with junk bonds in the 1970s and early 1980s—that's just what they're doing.

Bottom line: there's no such thing as a good or bad idea regardless of price!

"THE MOST IMPORTANT THING," JULY 1, 2003

JOEL GREENBLATT: *Individual investors need to think of this "most important" point with every investment decision. No matter how good an investment sounds, if price has not yet been considered, you can't know if it is a good investment.*

~

It's a fundamental premise of the efficient market hypothesis—and it makes perfect sense—that if you buy something for its fair value, you can expect a return that is fair given the risk. But active investors aren't in it for fair risk-adjusted returns; they want superior returns. (If you'll be satisfied with fair returns, why not invest passively in an index fund and save a lot of trouble?) So buying something at its intrinsic value is no great shakes. And paying *more* than something's worth is clearly a mistake; it takes a lot of hard work or a lot of luck to turn something bought at a too-high price into a successful investment.

Remember the Nifty Fifty investing I described in the last chapter? At their highs, many of those stalwart companies sported price/earnings ratios (the ratio of the stock's price to the earnings behind each share) between 80 and 90. (For comparison, the postwar average price/earnings ratio for stocks in general has been in the midteens.) None of their partisans appeared to be worried about those elevated valuations.

Then, in just a few years, everything changed. In the early 1970s, the stock market cooled off, exogenous factors like the oil embargo and rising inflation clouded the picture and the Nifty Fifty stocks collapsed. Within a few years, those price/earnings ratios of 80 or 90 had fallen to 8 or 9, meaning investors in America's best companies had lost 90 percent of their money. People may have bought into great companies, but they paid the wrong price.

At Oaktree we say, "Well bought is half sold." By this we mean we don't spend a lot of time thinking about what price we're going to be able to sell a holding for, or when, or to whom, or through what mechanism. If you've bought it cheap, eventually those questions will answer themselves.

JOEL GREENBLATT: *Many value investors are not good at knowing when to sell (and many sell way too early). However, knowing when to buy cures many of the mistakes resulting from selling too early.*

If your estimate of intrinsic value is correct, over time an asset's price should converge with its value.

JOEL GREENBLATT: *Keeping this statement in mind, that the market eventually gets it right, is one of the most important things to remember when the market acts emotionally over the short term.*

What are the companies worth? Eventually, this is what it comes down to. It's not enough to buy a share in a good idea, or even a good business. You must buy it at a reasonable (or, hopefully, a bargain) price.

"BUBBLE.COM," JANUARY 3, 2000

∼

All of this begs the question, what goes into the price? What should a prospective buyer be looking at to be sure the price is right? Underlying fundamental value, of course, but most of the time a security's price will be affected at least as much—and its short-term fluctuations determined primarily—by two other factors: psychology and technicals.

Most investors—and certainly most nonprofessionals—know little about technicals. These are nonfundamental factors—that is, things unrelated to value—that affect the supply and demand for securities. Two examples: the forced selling that takes place when market crashes cause levered investors to receive margin calls and be sold out, and the inflows of cash to mutual funds that require portfolio managers to buy. In both cases, people are forced to enter into securities transactions without much regard for price.

Believe me, there's nothing better than buying from someone who has to sell regardless of price during a crash. Many of the best buys we've ever made occurred for that reason. A couple of observations are in order, however:

- You can't make a career out of buying from forced sellers and selling to forced buyers; they're not around all the time, just on rare occasions at the extremes of crises and bubbles.
- Since buying from a forced seller is the best thing in our world, *being* a forced seller is the worst. That means it's essential to arrange your affairs so you'll be able to hold on—and not sell—at the worst of times. This requires both long-term capital and strong psychological resources.

JOEL GREENBLATT: *For an individual investor this means that if you have invested too much in the market or in a particular investment and you can't take the pain during periods of downside volatility, you can create a situation where you are the forced seller that Marks talks about here.*

And that brings me to the second factor that exerts such a powerful influence on price: psychology. It's impossible to overstate how important this is. In fact, it's so vital that several later chapters are devoted to discussing investor psychology and how to deal with its manifestations.

Whereas the key to ascertaining value is skilled financial analysis, the key to understanding the price/value relationship—and the outlook for it—lies largely in insight into other investors' minds. Investor psychology can cause a security to be priced just about anywhere in the short run, regardless of its fundamentals.

JOEL GREENBLATT: *Once again, as Buffett would say, the best investment class would teach how to estimate value and then how to think about market prices. Merely understanding that prices can deviate wildly from value over the short run is key. Understanding psychology so that you can take advantage of these deviations when they appear is the hard part.*

The discipline that is most important is not accounting or economics, but psychology.

The key is who likes the investment now and who doesn't. Future price changes will be determined by whether it comes to be liked by more people or fewer people in the future.

Investing is a popularity contest, and the most dangerous thing is to buy something at the peak of its popularity. At that point, all favorable facts and opinions are already factored into its price, and no new buyers are left to emerge.

HOWARD MARKS: *The second key theme isn't "the most important thing," but "the riskiest things." The book, preoccupied with risk as it is, describes a large number of things that make investing perilous. Pulling them together through these annotations should help you recognize them and thus avoid them. The biggest losers—be they Nifty-Fifty stocks in 1969, Internet stocks in 1999, or mortgage vehicles in 2006—had something in common: no one could find a flaw. There are lots of ways to describe this condition: "priced for perfection," "on the pedestal of popularity," and "nothing can go wrong." Nothing's perfect, however, and everything eventually turns out to have flaws. When you pay for perfection, you don't get what you expected, and the high price you pay exposes you to risk of loss when reality comes to light. This is truly one of the riskiest things.*

The safest and most potentially profitable thing is to buy something when no one likes it. Given time, its popularity, and thus its price, can only go one way: up.

"RANDOM THOUGHTS ON THE IDENTIFICATION OF INVESTMENT OPPORTUNITIES," JANUARY 24, 1994

Clearly, this is yet another area that is (a) of critical importance and (b) extremely hard to master.

PAUL JOHNSON: *This comment is particularly important for students, as they tend to have limited experience.*

First, psychology is elusive. And second, the psychological factors that weigh on other investors' minds and influence their actions will weigh on yours as well. As you will read in later chapters, these forces tend to cause people to do the opposite of what a superior investor must do. For self-protection, then, you must invest the time and energy to understand market psychology.

HOWARD MARKS: *"The human side of investing" is the critical side. It's certainly an area in which superior investors must excel, since financial analysis won't guarantee superior performance if your reactions to developments are skewed by psychology just like those of others. Thus my third key theme relates to control over emotion and ego. Accomplishing this is quite difficult, since everything in the investing environment conspires to make investors do the wrong thing at the wrong time. We're all only human, so the challenge is to perform better than other investors even though we start with the same wiring.*

It's essential to understand that fundamental value will be only one of the factors determining a security's price on the day you buy it. Try to have psychology and technicals on your side as well.

~

The polar opposite of conscientious value investing is mindlessly chasing bubbles, in which the relationship between price and value is totally ignored.

All bubbles start with some nugget of truth:

- Tulips are beautiful and rare (in seventeenth-century Holland).
- The Internet is going to change the world.
- Real estate can keep up with inflation, and you can always live in a house.

A few clever investors figure out (or perhaps even foresee) these truths, invest in the asset, and begin to show profits. Then others catch on to the idea—or just notice that people are making money—and they buy as well, lifting the asset's price. But as the price rises further and investors become more inflamed by the possibility of easy money, they think less and less about whether the price is fair. It's an extreme rendition of the phenomenon I described earlier: people should like something less when its price rises, but in investing they often like it more.

JOEL GREENBLATT: *This is uncanny but often true. People are attracted to those investments that have performed well lately. They are also attracted to professional managers who have performed well lately, though there is usually not much correlation with that manager's future performance.*

In 2004–2006, for example, people could conjure up only good things about houses and condos: the desirability of participating in the American dream of home ownership; the ability to benefit from inflation; the fact that mortgage loans were cheap and payments would be tax deductible; and ultimately the accepted wisdom that "home prices only go up." We all know what happened to that little nugget of wisdom.

And what of that other infamous "can't lose" idea? In the tech bubble, buyers didn't worry about whether a stock was priced too high because they were sure someone else would be willing to pay them more for it. Unfortunately, the greater fool theory works only until it doesn't. Valuation eventually comes into play, and those who are holding the bag when it does have to face the music.

- The positives behind stocks can be genuine and still produce losses if you overpay for them.
- Those positives—and the massive profits that seemingly everyone else is enjoying—can eventually cause those who have resisted participating to capitulate and buy.
- A "top" in a stock, group or market occurs when the last hold-out who will become a buyer does so. The timing is often unrelated to fundamental developments.

- "Prices are too high" is far from synonymous with "the next move will be downward." Things can be overpriced and stay that way for a long time . . . or become far more so.
- Eventually, though, valuation has to matter.

///

JOEL GREENBLATT: *Read that final bullet again!*

PAUL JOHNSON: *These points are so very true, although challenging to master while engulfed in the endorphin rush of a mania or bubble.*

\\

"BUBBLE.COM," JANUARY 3, 2000

The problem is that in bubbles, "attractive" morphs into "attractive at any price." People often say, "It's not cheap, but I think it'll keep going up because of excess liquidity" (or any number of other reasons). In other words, they say, "It's fully priced, but I think it'll become more so." Buying or holding on that basis is extremely chancy, but that's what makes bubbles.

In bubbles, infatuation with market momentum takes over from any notion of value and fair price, and greed (plus the pain of standing by as others make seemingly easy money) neutralizes any prudence that might otherwise hold sway.

To sum up, I believe that an investment approach based on solid value is the most dependable. In contrast, counting on others to give you a profit regardless of value—relying on a bubble—is probably the least.

~

Consider the possible routes to investment profit:

- *Benefiting from a rise in the asset's intrinsic value.* The problem is that increases in value are hard to predict accurately. Further, the conventional view of the potential for increase is usually baked into the asset's price, meaning that unless your view is different from the consensus and superior, it's likely you're already paying for the potential improvement.

  In certain areas of investing—most notably private equity (the buying of companies) and real estate—"control investors" can strive to create increases in value through active management of the asset. This is worth doing, but it's time-consuming and uncertain and requires considerable expertise. And it can be hard to bring about improvement, for example, in an already good company.

- *Applying leverage.* Here the problem is that using leverage—buying with borrowed money—doesn't make anything a better investment or increase the probability of gains. It merely magnifies whatever gains or losses may materialize. And it introduces the risk of ruin if a portfolio fails to satisfy a contractual value test and lenders can demand their money back at a time when prices and illiquidity are depressed. Over the years leverage has been associated with high returns, but also with the most spectacular meltdowns and crashes.

PAUL JOHNSON: *This is one of the most important comments in chapter 4. This is a lesson that all young investors fail to learn at their own peril.*

- *Selling for more than your asset's worth.* Everyone hopes a buyer will come along who's willing to overpay for what they have for sale. But certainly the hoped-for arrival of this sucker can't be counted on. Unlike having an underpriced asset move to its fair value, expecting appreciation on the part of a fairly priced or overpriced asset requires irrationality on the part of buyers that absolutely cannot be considered dependable.
- *Buying something for less than its value.* In my opinion, this is what it's all about—the most dependable way to make money. Buying at a discount from intrinsic value and having the asset's price move toward its value doesn't require serendipity; it just requires that market participants wake up to reality. When the market's functioning properly, value exerts a magnetic pull on price.

JOEL GREENBLATT: *Eventually, the market does operate and get it "right." Read Marks's statement again; it is an incredibly useful image.*

PAUL JOHNSON: *Here, Marks articulates the simple beauty behind value investing. Buying at the right price is the hard part of the exercise. Once done correctly, time and other market participants take care of the rest.*

Of all the possible routes to investment profit, buying cheap is clearly the most reliable. Even that, however, isn't sure to work. You can be wrong about the current value. Or events can come along that reduce value. Or deterioration in attitudes or markets can make something sell even further below its value. Or the convergence of price and intrinsic value can take more time than you have; as John Maynard Keynes pointed out, "The market can remain irrational longer than you can remain solvent."

HOWARD MARKS: *Fear of looking wrong: It comes as quite a shock to many new investors how long it can take for even correct judgments to work out. One of the most important roles of your strong view of intrinsic value is as a foundation for conviction: to help you hang in until the market comes to agree with you and prices the asset where it should.*

Trying to buy below value isn't infallible, but it's the best chance we have.

5

The Most Important Thing Is . . . Understanding Risk

Investing consists of exactly one thing: dealing with the future. And because none of us can know the future with certainty, risk is inescapable. Thus, dealing with risk is an essential—I think *the* essential—element in investing. It's not hard to find investments that might go up. If you can find enough of these, you'll have moved in the right direction. But you're unlikely to succeed for long if you haven't dealt explicitly with risk. The first step consists of understanding it. The second step is recognizing when it's high. The critical final step is controlling it. Because the issue is so complex and so important, I devote three chapters to examining risk in depth.

PAUL JOHNSON: *Marks's discussion of risk in chapters 5, 6, and 7 is the most comprehensive and complete I have ever seen in an investment book. Furthermore, his is the best articulation of risk I have encountered in any discussion or publication. These three chapters are the highlight of the book for me.*

Why do I say risk assessment is such an essential element in the investment process? There are three powerful reasons.

First, risk is a bad thing, and most level-headed people want to avoid or minimize it. It is an underlying assumption in financial theory that people are naturally risk-averse, meaning they'd rather take less risk than more. Thus, for starters, an investor considering a given investment has to make judgments about how risky it is and whether he or she can live with the absolute quantum of risk.

Second, when you're considering an investment, your decision should be a function of the risk entailed as well as the potential return. Because of their dislike for risk, investors have to be bribed with higher prospective returns to take incremental risks. Put simply, if both a U.S. Treasury note and small company stock appeared likely to return 7 percent per year, everyone would rush to buy the former (driving up its price and reducing its prospective return) and dump the latter (driving down its price and thus increasing its return). This process of adjusting relative prices, which economists call *equilibration,* is supposed to render prospective returns proportional to risk.

So, going beyond determining whether he or she can bear the absolute amount of risk that is attendant, the investor's second job is to determine whether the return on a given investment justifies taking the risk. Clearly, return tells just half of the story, and risk assessment is required.

Third, when you consider investment results, the return means only so much by itself; the risk taken has to be assessed as well. Was the return achieved in safe instruments or risky ones? In fixed income securities or stocks? In large, established companies or smaller, shakier ones? In liquid stocks and bonds or illiquid private placements? With help from leverage or without it? In a concentrated portfolio or a diversified one?

Surely investors who get their statements and find that their accounts made 10 percent for the year don't know whether their money managers did a good job or a bad one. In order to reach a conclusion, they have to have some idea about how much risk their managers took. In other words, they have to have a feeling for "risk-adjusted return."

JOEL GREENBLATT: *However, many individual and institutional investor decisions are based on this number, which has little explanatory or predictive value.*

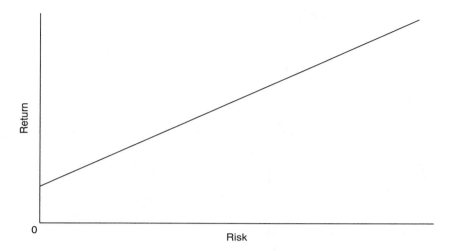

Figure 5.1

It is from the relationship between risk and return that arises the graphic representation that has become ubiquitous in the investment world (figure 5.1). It shows a "capital market line" that slopes upward to the right, indicating the positive relationship between risk and return. Markets set themselves up so that riskier assets appear to offer higher returns. If that weren't the case, who would buy them?

The familiar graph of the risk-return relationship is elegant in its simplicity. Unfortunately, many have drawn from it an erroneous conclusion that gets them into trouble.

Especially in good times, far too many people can be overheard saying, "Riskier investments provide higher returns. If you want to make more money, the answer is to take more risk." But riskier investments absolutely cannot be counted on to deliver higher returns. Why not? It's simple: if riskier investments reliably produced higher returns, they wouldn't be riskier!

The correct formulation is that in order to attract capital, riskier investments have to offer the prospect of higher returns, or higher promised returns, or higher expected returns. But there's

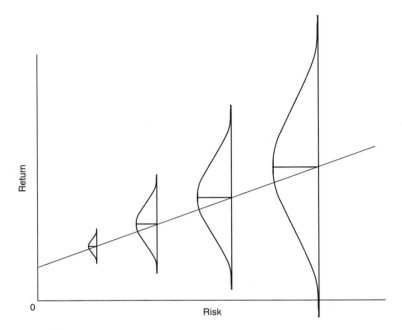

Figure 5.2

absolutely nothing to say those higher prospective returns have to materialize.

The way I conceptualize the capital market line makes it easier for me to relate to the relationship underlying it all (figure 5.2).

JOEL GREENBLATT: *This graph is a helpful way to visualize risk vs. return. Another helpful way to think about the probability distribution of future returns is to remember that the outcome distribution of these possible returns is not, in reality, normally distributed.*

HOWARD MARKS: *Investing requires us to deal with the future. If the future were knowable by all, investing wouldn't be very challenging (or, consequently, very profitable). Because it's not, my final key theme surrounds the importance of understanding uncertainty. The graphic above illustrates the essence of "riskier" investments. This isn't an abstraction; riskier investments involve greater uncertainty regarding the outcome, as well as the increased likelihood of some painful ones.*

Riskier investments are those for which the outcome is less certain. That is, the probability distribution of returns is wider. When priced fairly, riskier investments should entail:

- higher expected returns,
- the possibility of lower returns, and
- in some cases the possibility of losses.

The traditional risk/return graph (figure 5.1) is deceptive because it communicates the positive connection between risk and return but fails to suggest the uncertainty involved. It has brought a lot of people a lot of misery through its unwavering intimation that taking more risk leads to making more money.

I hope my version of the graph is more helpful.

PAUL JOHNSON: *Marks's discussion of the relationship between risk and return offers important clarity, particularly in this comparison of figures 5.1 and 5.2. The additional insight offered by figure 5.2 leads to a much clearer view of the proper way to relate risk and return than that presented in the more common figure 5.1.*

It's meant to suggest both the positive relationship between risk and expected return *and* the fact that uncertainty about the return and the possibility of loss increase as risk increases.

"RISK," JANUARY 19, 2006

PAUL JOHNSON: *So well said! Marks's dismissal of risk's equaling volatility, favored by academics and some practitioners, is excellent. Instead, Marks offers a much more insightful definition of risk.*

JOEL GREENBLATT: *Comparing the risk of permanent loss of capital to potential reward is one of the most important concepts in investing. Yet Marks points out that many academic versions of risk, which are merely the measure of volatility relative to returns, miss much of the point. They do not reflect most investors' perception of risk.*

~

Our next major task is to define risk. What exactly does it involve? We can get an idea from its synonyms: danger, hazard, jeopardy, peril. They all sound like reasonable candidates, and pretty undesirable.

And yet, finance theory (the same theory that contributed the risk-return graph shown in figure 5.1 and the concept of risk-adjustment) defines risk very precisely as volatility (or variability or deviation). None of these conveys the necessary sense of "peril."

According to the academicians who developed capital market theory, risk equals volatility, because volatility indicates the un-reliability of an investment. I take great issue with this definition of risk.

It's my view that—knowingly or unknowingly—academicians settled on volatility as the proxy for risk as a matter of convenience. They needed a number for their calculations that was objective and could be ascertained historically and extrapolated into the future. Volatility fits the bill, and most of the other types of risk do not. The problem with all of this, however, is that I just don't think volatility is the risk most investors care about.

There are many kinds of risk. . . . But volatility may be the least relevant of them all. Theory says investors demand more return from investments that are more volatile. But for the market to set the prices for investments such that more volatile investments will appear likely to produce higher returns, there have to be people demanding that relationship, and I haven't met them yet. I've never heard anyone at Oaktree—or anywhere else, for that matter—say, "I won't buy it, because its price might show big fluctuations," or "I won't buy it, because it might have a down quarter." Thus, it's hard for me to believe volatility is the risk investors factor in when setting prices and prospective returns.

Rather than volatility, I think people decline to make investments primarily because they're worried about a loss of capital or an unacceptably low return. To me, "I need more upside potential because I'm afraid I could lose money" makes an awful lot more sense than "I need more upside potential because I'm afraid the price may fluctuate." No, I'm sure "risk" is—first and foremost—the likelihood of losing money.

"RISK," JANUARY 19, 2006

The possibility of permanent loss is the risk I worry about, Oaktree worries about and every practical investor I know worries about.

///

PAUL JOHNSON: *I would go so far as to say that the risk of permanent capital loss is the only risk to worry about.*

\\

But there are many other kinds of risk, and you should be conscious of them, because they can either (a) affect you or (b) affect others and thus present you with opportunities for profit.

Investment risk comes in many forms. Many risks matter to some investors but not to others, and they may make a given investment seem safe for some investors but risky for others.

- *Falling short of one's goal*—Investors have differing needs, and for each investor the failure to meet those needs poses a risk. A retired executive may need 4 percent per year to pay the bills, whereas 6 percent would represent a windfall. But for a pension fund that has to average 8 percent per year, a prolonged period returning 6 percent would entail serious risk. Obviously this risk is personal and subjective, as opposed to absolute and objective. A given investment may be risky in this regard for some people but riskless for others. Thus this cannot be the risk for which "the market" demands compensation in the form of higher prospective returns.
- *Underperformance*—Let's say an investment manager knows there won't be more money forthcoming no matter how well a client's account performs, but it's clear the account will be lost if it fails to keep up with some index. That's "benchmark risk," and the manager can eliminate it by emulating the index. But every investor who's unwilling to throw in the towel on

outperformance, and who chooses to deviate from the index in its pursuit, will have periods of significant underperformance. In fact, since many of the best investors stick most strongly to their approach—and since no approach will work all the time—the best investors can have some of the greatest periods of underperformance. Specifically, in crazy times, disciplined investors willingly accept the risk of not taking enough risk to keep up. (See Warren Buffett and Julian Robertson in 1999. That year, underperformance was a badge of courage because it denoted a refusal to participate in the tech bubble.)

///

JOEL GREENBLATT: *In the decade of the 2000s, 79 percent of the investment managers who ended up in the top quartile of performance spent at least three years in the bottom quartile (source: Davis Advisors). Most investors chase the hot fund and don't stick with managers who underperform over the short term.*

\\

- *Career risk*—This is the extreme form of underperformance risk: the risk that arises when the people who manage money and the people whose money it is are different people. In those cases, the managers (or "agents") may not care much about gains, in which they won't share, but may be deathly afraid of losses that could cost them their jobs. The implication is clear: risk that could jeopardize return to an agent's firing point is rarely worth taking.
- *Unconventionality*—Along similar lines, there's the risk of being different. Stewards of other people's money can be more comfortable turning in average performance, regardless of where it stands in absolute terms, than with the possibility that unconventional actions will prove unsuccessful and get them fired. . . . Concern over this risk keeps many people from superior results, but it also creates opportunities in unorthodox investments for those who dare to be different.
- *Illiquidity*—If an investor needs money with which to pay for surgery in three months or buy a home in a year, he or she may be unable to make an investment that can't be counted on for liquidity that meets the schedule. Thus, for this investor, risk isn't

just losing money or volatility, or any of the above. It's being unable when needed to turn an investment into cash at a reasonable price. This, too, is a personal risk.

"RISK," JANUARY 19, 2006

~

Now I want to spend a little time on the subject of what gives rise to the risk of loss.

First, risk of loss does not necessarily stem from weak fundamentals. A fundamentally weak asset—a less-than-stellar company's stock, a speculative-grade bond or a building in the wrong part of town—can make for a very successful investment if bought at a low-enough price.

Second, risk can be present even without weakness in the macroenvironment. The combination of arrogance, failure to understand and allow for risk, and a small adverse development can be enough to wreak havoc. It can happen to anyone who doesn't spend the time and effort required to understand the processes underlying his or her portfolio.

Mostly it comes down to psychology that's too positive and thus prices that are too high. Investors tend to associate exciting stories and pizzazz with high potential returns. They also expect high returns from things that have been doing well lately. These souped-up investments may deliver on people's expectations for a while, but they certainly entail high risk. Having been borne aloft on the crowd's excitement and elevated to what I call the "pedestal of popularity," they offer the possibility of continued high returns, but also of low or negative ones.

HOWARD MARKS: *The riskiest things: The most dangerous investment conditions generally stem from psychology that's too positive. For this reason, fundamentals don't have to deteriorate in order for losses to occur; a downgrading of investor opinion will suffice. High prices often collapse of their own weight.*

Theory says high return is associated with high risk because the former exists to compensate for the latter. But pragmatic value investors feel just the opposite: They believe high return and low risk can be achieved simultaneously by buying things for less than they're worth. In the same way, overpaying implies both low return and high risk.

Dull, ignored, possibly tarnished and beaten-down securities—often bargains exactly because they haven't been performing well—are often the ones value investors favor for high returns. Their returns in bull markets are rarely at the top of the heap, but their performance is generally excellent on average, more consistent than that of "hot" stocks and characterized by low variability, low fundamental risk and smaller losses when markets do badly. Much of the time, the greatest risk in these low-luster bargains lies in the possibility of underperforming in heated bull markets. That's something the risk-conscious value investor is willing to live with.

~

I'm sure we agree that investors should and do demand higher prospective returns on the investments they perceive as riskier. And hopefully we can agree that losing money is the risk people care about most in demanding prospective returns and thus in setting prices for investments. An important question remains: *how do they measure that risk?*

First, it clearly is nothing but a matter of opinion: hopefully an educated, skillful estimate of the future, but still just an estimate.

Second, the standard for quantification is nonexistent. With any given investment, some people will think the risk is high and others will think it's low. Some will state it as the probability of not making money, and some as the probability of losing a given fraction of their money (and so forth). Some will think of it as the risk of losing money over one year, and some as the risk of losing money over the entire holding period. Clearly, even if all the investors involved met in a room and showed their cards, they'd never agree on a single number representing an investment's riskiness. And even if they could, that number wouldn't likely be capable of being compared against another number, set by another group of investors, for another investment. This is one of the reasons why I say risk and the risk/return decision aren't "machinable," or capable of being turned over to a computer.

Ben Graham and David Dodd put it this way more than sixty years ago in the second edition of *Security Analysis*, the bible of value investors: "the relation between different kinds of investments and the risk of loss is entirely too indefinite, and too variable with changing conditions, to permit of sound mathematical formulation."

Third, risk is deceptive. Conventional considerations are easy to factor in, like the likelihood that normally recurring events will recur. But freakish, once-in-a-lifetime events are hard to quantify. The fact that an investment is susceptible to a particularly serious risk that will occur infrequently if at all—what I call the *improbable disaster*—means it can seem safer than it really is.

The bottom line is that, looked at prospectively, much of risk is subjective, hidden and unquantifiable.

Where does that leave us? If the risk of loss can't be measured, quantified or even observed—and if it's consigned to subjectivity—how can it be dealt with? Skillful investors can get a sense for the risk present in a given situation. They make that judgment primarily based on (a) the stability and dependability of value and (b) the relationship between price and value. Other things will enter into their thinking, but most will be subsumed under these two.

There have been many efforts of late to make risk assessment more scientific. Financial institutions routinely employ quantitative "risk managers" separate from their asset management teams and have adopted computer models such as "value at risk" to measure the risk in a portfolio. But the results produced by these people and their tools will be no better than the inputs they rely on and the judgments they make about how to process the inputs. In my opinion, they'll never be as good as the best investors' subjective judgments.

Given the difficulty of quantifying the probability of loss, investors who want some objective measure of risk-adjusted return—and they are many—can only look to the so-called Sharpe ratio. This is the ratio of a portfolio's excess return (its return above the "riskless rate," or the rate on short-term Treasury bills) to the standard deviation of the return. This calculation seems serviceable for public market securities that trade and price often; there is some logic, and it truly is the best we have. While it says nothing explicitly about the likelihood of loss, there may be reason to believe that the prices of fundamentally riskier securities fluctuate more than those of safer ones, and thus that the Sharpe ratio has some relevance.

JOEL GREENBLATT: *In a similar light, a Sortino ratio looks at only downside volatility rather than both upside and downside volatility. However, neither measure does a good job of measuring risk of future loss.*

For private assets lacking market prices—like real estate and whole companies—there's no alternative to subjective risk adjustment.

~

A few years ago, while considering the difficulty of measuring risk prospectively, I realized that because of its latent, nonquantitative and subjective nature, the risk of an investment—defined as the likelihood of loss—can't be measured in retrospect any more than it can a priori.

Let's say you make an investment that works out as expected. Does that mean it wasn't risky? Maybe you buy something for $100 and sell it a year later for $200. Was it risky? Who knows? Perhaps it exposed you to great potential uncertainties that didn't materialize. Thus, its real riskiness might have been high. Or let's say the investment produces a loss. Does that mean it was risky? Or that it should have been perceived as risky at the time it was analyzed and entered into?

If you think about it, the response to these questions is simple: The fact that something—in this case, loss—happened doesn't mean it was bound to happen, and the fact that something didn't happen doesn't mean it was unlikely.

Fooled by Randomness, by Nassim Nicholas Taleb, is the authority on this subject as far as I'm concerned, and in it he talks about the "alternative histories" that could have unfolded but didn't. There's more about this important book in chapter 16, but at the moment I am interested in how the idea of alternative histories relates to risk.

SETH KLARMAN: *This is where top-notch management may also make a difference. Astute managers will be aware of the many risks that could threaten their businesses and will take action to mitigate or avoid them. Poor managers will fail to notice risks or fail to act, thereby subjecting their firms to avoidable loss.*

In the investing world, one can live for years off one great coup or one extreme but eventually accurate forecast. But what's proved by one success? When markets are booming, the best results often go to those who take the most risk. Were they smart to anticipate good times and bulk up on beta, or just congenitally aggressive types who were bailed out by events? Most simply put, how often in our business are people right for the wrong reason? These are the people Nassim Nicholas Taleb calls "lucky idiots," and in the short run it's certainly hard to tell them from skilled investors.

The point is that even after an investment has been closed out, it's impossible to tell how much risk it entailed. Certainly the fact that an investment worked doesn't mean it wasn't risky, and vice versa. With regard to a successful investment, where do you look to learn whether the favorable outcome was inescapable or just one of a hundred possibilities (many of them unpleasant)? And ditto for a loser: how do we ascertain whether it was a reasonable but ill-fated venture, or just a wild stab that deserved to be punished?

Did the investor do a good job of assessing the risk entailed? That's another good question that's hard to answer. Need a model? Think of the weatherman. He says there's a 70 percent chance of rain tomorrow. It rains; was he right or wrong? Or it doesn't rain; was he right or wrong? It's impossible to assess the accuracy of probability estimates other than 0 and 100 except over a very large number of trials.

"RISK," JANUARY 19, 2006

And that brings me to the quotation from Elroy Dimson that led off this chapter: "Risk means more things can happen than will happen." Now we move toward the metaphysical aspects of risk.

HOWARD MARKS: *Understanding uncertainty: Dimson's formulation reminds us of a very simple concept: that many things are possible in the future. We can't know which of the possibilities will occur, and this uncertainty contributes to the challenge of investing. "Single-scenario" investors ignore this fact, oversimplify the task, and need fortuitous outcomes to produce good results.*

Perhaps you recall the opening sentence of this chapter: Investing consists of exactly one thing: dealing with the future. Yet clearly it's impossible to "know" anything about the future. If we're farsighted we can have an idea of the range of future outcomes and their relative likelihood of occurring—that is, we can fashion a rough probability distribution. (On the other hand, if we're not, we won't know these things and it'll be pure guesswork.)

> **HOWARD MARKS:** *Understanding uncertainty: The possibility of a variety of outcomes means we mustn't think of the future in terms of a single result but rather as a range of possibilities. The best we can do is fashion a probability distribution that summarizes the possibilities and describes their relative likelihood. We must think about the full range, not just the ones that are most likely to materialize. Some of the greatest losses arise when investors ignore the improbable possibilities.*

If we have a sense for the future, we'll be able to say which outcome is most likely, what other outcomes also have a good chance of occurring, how broad the range of possible outcomes is and thus what the "expected result" is. The expected result is calculated by weighting each outcome by its probability of occurring; it's a figure that says a lot—but not everything—about the likely future.

But even when we know the shape of the probability distribution, which outcome is most likely and what the expected result is—and even if our expectations are reasonably correct—we know about only likelihoods or tendencies. I've spent hours playing gin and backgammon with my good friend Bruce Newberg. Our time spent with cards and dice, where the odds are absolutely knowable, demonstrates the significant role played by randomness, and thus the vagary of probabilities. Bruce has put it admirably into words: "There's a big difference between probability and outcome. Probable things fail to happen—and improbable things happen—all the time." That's one of the most important things you can know about investment risk.

> **JOEL GREENBLATT:** *When thinking about a portfolio of investments, one thing to keep in mind is that the correlation of these improbable occurrences can affect many of your investments at the same time.*

While on the subject of probability distributions, I want to take a moment to make special mention of the normal distribution. Obviously investors are required to make judgments about future events. To do that, we settle on a central value around which we think events are likely to cluster. This may be the mean or expected value (the outcome that on average is expected to occur), the median (the outcome with half the possibilities above and half below) or the mode (the single most likely outcome). But to cope with the future it's not sufficient to have a central expectation; we have to have a sense for the other possible outcomes and their likelihood. We need a distribution that describes all of the possibilities.

Most phenomena that cluster around a central value—for example, the heights of people—form the familiar bell-shaped curve, with the probability of a given observation peaking at the center and trailing off toward the extremes, or "tails." There may be more men of five feet ten inches than any other height, somewhat fewer of five feet nine inches or five feet eleven inches, a lot less of five feet three inches or six feet five inches, and almost none of four feet eight inches or seven feet. Rather than enumerating the probability of each observation individually, standard distributions provide a convenient way to summarize the probabilities, such that a few statistics can tell you everything you have to know about the shape of things to come.

The most common bell-shaped distribution is called the "normal" distribution. However, people often use the terms *bell-shaped* and *normal* interchangeably, and they're not the same. The former is a general type of distribution, while the latter is a specific bell-shaped distribution with very definite statistical properties. Failure to distinguish between the two doubtless made an important contribution to the recent credit crisis.

In the years leading up to the crisis, financial engineers, or "quants," played a big part in creating and evaluating financial products such as derivatives and structured entities. In many cases they made the assumption that future events would be normally distributed. But the normal distribution assumes events in the distant tails will happen extremely infrequently, while the distribution of financial developments—shaped by humans, with their tendency to go to emotion-driven extremes of behavior—should probably be seen as having "fatter" tails. Thus, when widespread mortgage defaults began to occur, events thought to be unlikely befell mortgage-related vehicles on a regular basis. Investors in vehicles that had been constructed on the basis of normal distributions, without much allowance for "tail events" (some might borrow Nassim Nicholas Taleb's term "black swans"), often saw the wheels come off.

Now that investing has become so reliant on higher math, we have to be on the lookout for occasions when people wrongly apply simplifying assumptions to a complex world. Quantification often lends excessive authority to statements that should be taken with a grain of salt. That creates significant potential for trouble.

$\sim$

Here's the key to understanding risk: it's largely a matter of opinion. It's hard to be definitive about risk, even after the fact. You can see that one investor lost less than another in bad times and conclude that that investor took less risk. Or you can note that one investment declined more than another in a given environment and thus say it was riskier. Are these statements necessarily accurate?

For the most part, I think it's fair to say that investment performance is what happens when a set of developments—geopolitical, macro-economic, company-level, technical and psychological—collide with an extant portfolio. Many futures are possible, to paraphrase Dimson, but only one future occurs. The future you get may be beneficial to your portfolio or harmful, and that may be attributable to your foresight, prudence or luck.

PAUL JOHNSON: *Fully understanding this insight will be a major step toward understanding investment performance and has important philosophical ramifications for investing.*

The performance of your portfolio under the one scenario that unfolds says nothing about how it would have fared under the many "alternative histories" that were possible.

- A portfolio can be set up to withstand 99 percent of all scenarios but succumb because it's the remaining 1 percent that materializes. Based on the outcome, it may seem to have been risky, whereas the investor might have been quite cautious.
- Another portfolio may be structured so that it will do very well in half the scenarios and very poorly in the other half. But if the desired environment materializes and it prospers, onlookers can conclude that it was a low-risk portfolio.
- The success of a third portfolio can be entirely contingent on one oddball development, but if it occurs, wild aggression can be mistaken for conservatism and foresight.

Return alone—and especially return over short periods of time—says very little about the quality of investment decisions. Return has to be evaluated relative to the amount of risk taken to achieve it. And yet, risk cannot be measured. Certainly it cannot be gauged on the basis of what "everybody" says at a moment in time. Risk can be judged only by sophisticated, experienced second-level thinkers.

∾

Here's my wrap-up on understanding risk:

Investment risk is largely invisible before the fact—except perhaps to people with unusual insight—and even after an investment has been exited. For this reason, many of the great financial disasters we've seen have been failures to foresee and manage risk. There are several reasons for this.

- Risk exists only in the future, and it's impossible to know for sure what the future holds. . . . No ambiguity is evident when we view the past. Only the things that happened, happened. But that definiteness doesn't mean the process that creates outcomes is clear-cut and dependable. Many things could have happened in each case in the past, and the fact that only one did happen understates the variability that existed.
- Decisions whether or not to bear risk are made in contemplation of normal patterns recurring, and they do most of the time. But once in a while, something very different happens. . . . Occasionally, the improbable does occur.
- Projections tend to cluster around historic norms and call for only small changes. . . . The point is, people usually expect the future to be like the past and underestimate the potential for change.
- We hear a lot about "worst-case" projections, but they often turn out not to be negative enough. I tell my father's story of the gambler who lost regularly. One day he heard about a race with only one horse in it, so he bet the rent money. Halfway around the track, the horse jumped over the fence and ran away. Invariably things can get worse than people expect. Maybe "worst-case" means "the worst we've seen in the past." But that doesn't mean things can't be worse in the future. In 2007, many people's worst-case assumptions were exceeded.

- Risk shows up lumpily. If we say "2 percent of mortgages default" each year, and even if that's true when we look at a multi-year average, an unusual spate of defaults can occur at a point in time, sinking a structured finance vehicle. It's invariably the case that some investors—especially those who employ high leverage—will fail to survive at those intervals.

- People overestimate their ability to gauge risk and understand mechanisms they've never before seen in operation. In theory, one thing that distinguishes humans from other species is that we can figure out that something's dangerous without experiencing it. We don't have to burn ourselves to know we shouldn't sit on a hot stove. But in bullish times, people tend not to perform this function. Rather than recognize risk ahead, they tend to overestimate their ability to understand how new financial inventions will work.

- Finally and importantly, most people view risk taking primarily as a way to make money. Bearing higher risk generally produces higher returns. The market has to set things up to look like that'll be the case; if it didn't, people wouldn't make risky investments. But it can't always work that way, or else risky investments wouldn't be risky. And when risk bearing doesn't work, it *really* doesn't work, and people are reminded what risk's all about.

"NO DIFFERENT THIS TIME," DECEMBER 17, 2007

HOWARD MARKS: *Understanding uncertainty: Investing requires us to make decisions about the future. Usually we do so by assuming it will bear a resemblance to the past. But that's far from saying outcomes will be distributed the same as always. Unusual and unlikely things can happen, and outcomes can occur in runs (and go to extremes) that are hard to predict. Underestimating uncertainty and its consequences is a big contributor to investor difficulty.*

6

The Most Important Thing Is . . . Recognizing Risk

Great investing requires both generating returns and controlling risk. And recognizing risk is an absolute prerequisite for controlling it.

Hopefully I've made clear what I think risk is (and isn't). Risk means uncertainty about which outcome will occur and about the possibility of loss when the unfavorable ones do.

PAUL JOHNSON: *This is the clearest and most accurate definition of risk I have heard. Marks nails it with this statement.*

The next important step is to describe the process through which risk can be recognized for what it is.

Recognizing risk often starts with understanding when investors are paying it too little heed, being too optimistic and paying too much for a given asset as a result. High risk, in other words, comes primarily with high prices. Whether it be an individual security or other asset that is overrated and thus overpriced, or an entire market that's been borne aloft by bullish sentiment and thus is sky-high, participating when prices are high rather than shying away is the main source of risk.

JOEL GREENBLATT: *Paying too much is a great way to lose money regardless of other measures of risk, such as volatility or degree of diversification.*

HOWARD MARKS: *The riskiest things: The greatest risk doesn't come from low quality or high volatility. It comes from paying prices that are too high. This isn't a theoretical risk; it's very real.*

Whereas the theorist thinks return and risk are two separate things, albeit correlated, the value investor thinks of high risk and low prospective return as nothing but two sides of the same coin, both stemming primarily from high prices.

CHRISTOPHER DAVIS: *That is, high price both increases risk and lowers returns.*

Thus, awareness of the relationship between price and value—whether for a single security or an entire market—is an essential component of dealing successfully with risk.

JOEL GREENBLATT: *The risk of misvaluing an investment is a component of this thought process for the value investor.*

Risk arises when markets go so high that prices imply losses rather than the potential rewards they should. Dealing with this risk starts with recognizing it.

All along the upward-sloping capital market line, the increase in potential return represents compensation for bearing incremental risk. Except for those people who can generate "alpha" or access managers who have it, investors shouldn't plan on getting added return without bearing incremental risk. And for doing so, they should demand risk premiums.

But at some point in the swing of the pendulum, people usually forget that truth and embrace risk taking to excess. In short, in bull markets—usually when things have been going well for a while—people tend to say, "Risk is my friend. The more risk I take, the greater my return will be. I'd like more risk, please."

The truth is, risk tolerance is antithetical to successful investing. When people aren't afraid of risk, they'll accept risk without being compensated for doing so . . . and risk compensation will disappear.

HOWARD MARKS: *The riskiest things: Too-high prices come from investor psychology that's too positive, and too-high investor sentiment often stems from a dearth of risk aversion. Risk-averse investors are conscious of the potential for loss and demand compensation for bearing it—in the form of reasonable prices. When investors aren't sufficiently risk averse, they'll pay prices that are too high.*

This is a simple and inevitable relationship. When investors are unworried and risk-tolerant, they buy stocks at high price/earnings ratios and private companies at high multiples of EBITDA (cash flow, defined as earnings before interest, taxes, depreciation and amortization), and they pile into bonds despite narrow yield spreads and into real estate at minimal "cap rates" (the ratio of net operating income to price).

There are few things as risky as the widespread belief that there's no risk, because it's only when investors are suitably risk-averse that prospective returns will incorporate appropriate risk premiums.

CHRISTOPHER DAVIS: *A good analogy to this is the studies that show there are more traffic fatalities among drivers and passengers in SUVs than in compact cars despite SUVs' being bigger and more sturdily built. Drivers of SUVs believe they're not at risk in case of an accident, and this leads to riskier driving. The feeling of safety tends to increase risk while the awareness of risk tends to reduce it.*

HOWARD MARKS: *The riskiest things: "There are few things as risky as the widespread belief that there's no risk." The opening words of this paragraph are valuable because they highlight an excellent example of the ways investors' behavior creates the risks to which they are subjected. When they swallow worry-free beliefs, it truly is the riskiest thing.*

Hopefully in the future (a) investors will remember to fear risk and demand risk premiums and (b) we'll continue to be alert for times when they don't.

"SO MUCH THAT'S FALSE AND NUTTY," JULY 8, 2009

So a prime element in risk creation is a belief that risk is low, perhaps even gone altogether. That belief drives up prices and leads to the embrace of risky actions despite the lowness of prospective returns.

In 2005–2007, belief that risk had been banished caused prices to rise to bubble levels and investors to participate in what later turned out to be risky activities. This is one of the most dangerous of all processes, and its tendency to recur is remarkable.

HOWARD MARKS: *The riskiest things: A few times in my career, I've seen the rise of a belief that risk has been banished, cycles won't occur any longer, or the laws of economics have been suspended. The experienced, risk-conscious investor takes this as a sign of great danger.*

Of the many fairy tales told over the last few years, one of the most seductive—and thus dangerous—was the one about global risk reduction. It went this way:

- The risk of economic cycles has been eased by adroit central bank management.
- Because of globalization, risk has been spread worldwide rather than concentrated geographically.
- Securitization and syndication have distributed risk to many market participants rather than leaving it concentrated with just a few.
- Risk has been "tranched out" to the investors best able to bear it.
- Leverage has become less risky because interest rates and debt terms are so much more borrower-friendly.
- Leveraged buyouts are safer because the companies being bought are fundamentally stronger.
- Risk can be hedged through long/short and absolute return investing or the use of derivatives designed for that purpose.
- Improvements in computers, mathematics and modeling have made the markets better understood and thus less risky.

An apt metaphor came from *Pension & Investments* (August 20, 2007): "Jill Fredston is a nationally recognized avalanche expert. . . . She knows about a kind of moral hazard risk, where better safety gear can entice climbers to take more risk—making them in fact less safe."

JOEL GREENBLATT: *This is such an important thought when assessing the true benefits of different methods of diversification.*

Like opportunities to make money, the degree of risk present in a market derives from the behavior of the participants, not from securities, strategies and institutions. Regardless of what's designed into market structures, risk will be low only if investors behave prudently.

The bottom line is that tales like this one about risk control rarely turn out to be true. Risk cannot be eliminated; it just gets transferred and spread. And developments that make the world look less risky usually are illusory, and thus in presenting a rosy picture they tend to make the world more risky. These are among the important lessons of 2007.

"NOW IT'S ALL BAD," SEPTEMBER 10, 2007

The risk-is-gone myth is one of the most dangerous sources of risk, and a major contributor to any bubble. At the extreme of the pendulum's upswing, the belief that risk is low and that the investment in question is sure to produce profits intoxicates the herd and causes its members to forget caution, worry and fear of loss, and instead to obsess about the risk of missing opportunity.

HOWARD MARKS: *The riskiest things: In the summer of 2009, the New York Times asked a dozen people to write about the causes of the crisis. My response, published on dealbook.com on October 5, 2009, was entitled "Too Much Trust, Too Little Worry." Take a look, and note that carefree, unworried investors are their own worst enemy.*

The recent crisis came about primarily because investors partook of novel, complex and dangerous things, in greater amounts than ever before. They took on too much leverage and committed too much capital to illiquid investments. Why did they do these things? It all happened because investors believed too much, worried too little and thus took too much risk. In short, they believed they were living in a low-risk world. . . .

Worry and its relatives, distrust, skepticism and risk aversion, are essential ingredients in a safe financial system. Worry keeps risky loans from being made, companies from taking on more debt than they can service, portfolios from becoming overly concentrated, and unproven schemes from turning into popular manias. When worry and risk aversion are present as they should be, investors will question, investigate and act prudently. Risky investments either won't be undertaken or will be required to provide adequate compensation in terms of anticipated return.

But only when investors are sufficiently risk-averse will markets offer adequate risk premiums. When worry is in short supply, risky borrowers and questionable schemes will have easy access to capital, and the financial system will become precarious. Too much money will chase the risky and the new, driving up asset prices and driving down prospective returns and safety.

Clearly, in the months and years leading up to the crisis, few participants worried as much as they're supposed to.

"TOUCHSTONES," NOVEMBER 10, 2009

~

Investment risk comes primarily from too-high prices, and too-high prices often come from excessive optimism and inadequate skepticism and risk aversion. Contributing underlying factors can include low prospective returns on safer investments, recent good performance by risky ones, strong inflows of capital, and easy availability of credit. The key lies in understanding what impact things like these are having.

The investment thought process is a chain in which each investment sets the requirement for the next. Here's how I described the process in 2004:

I'll use a "typical" market of a few years back to illustrate how this works in real life: The interest rate on the thirty-day T-bill might have been 4 percent. So investors say, "If I'm going to go out five years, I want 5 percent. And to buy the ten-year note I have to get 6 percent." Investors demand a higher rate to extend maturity because they're concerned about the risk to purchasing power, a risk that is assumed to increase with time to maturity. That's why the yield curve, which in reality is a portion of the capital market line, normally slopes upward with the increase in asset life.

Now let's factor in credit risk. "If the ten-year Treasury pays 6 percent, I'm not going to buy a ten-year single-A corporate unless I'm promised 7 percent." This introduces the concept of credit spreads. Our hypothetical investor wants 100 basis points to go from a "guvvie" to a "corporate." If the consensus of investors feels the same, that's what the spread will be.

What if we depart from investment-grade bonds? "I'm not going to touch a high yield bond unless I get 600 over a Treasury note of comparable maturity." So high yield bonds are required to yield 12 percent, for a spread of 6 percent over the Treasury note, if they're going to attract buyers.

Now let's leave fixed income altogether. Things get tougher, because you can't look anywhere to find the prospective return on investments like stocks (that's because, simply put, their returns are conjectural, not "fixed"). But investors have a sense for these things. "Historically S&P stocks have returned 10 percent, and I'll buy them only if I think they're going to keep doing so. . . . And riskier stocks should return more; I won't buy on the NASDAQ unless I think I'm going to get 13 percent."

From there it's onward and upward. "If I can get 10 percent from stocks, I need 15 percent to accept the illiquidity and uncertainty associated with real estate. And 25 percent if I'm going to invest in buyouts . . . and 30 percent to induce me to go for venture capital, with its low success ratio."

That's the way it's supposed to work, and in fact I think it generally does (although the requirements aren't the same at all times). The result is a capital market line of the sort that has become familiar to many of us, as shown in figure 6.1.

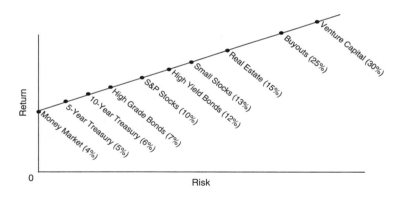

Figure 6.1

A big problem for investment returns today stems from the starting point for this process: The riskless rate isn't 4 percent; it's closer to 1 percent. . . .

Typical investors still want more return if they're going to accept time risk, but with the starting point at 1+ percent, now

4 percent is the right rate for the ten-year (not 6 percent). They won't go into stocks unless they get 6 to 7 percent. And junk bonds may not be worth it at yields below 7 percent. Real estate has to yield 8 percent or so. For buyouts to be attractive they have to appear to promise 15 percent, and so on. Thus, we now have a capital market line like the one shown in figure 6.2, which is (a) at a much lower level and (b) much flatter.

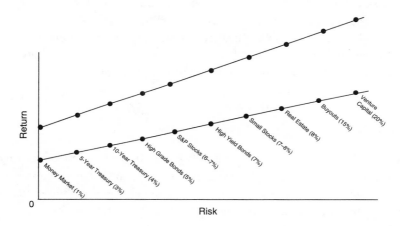

Figure 6.2

The lower level of the line is explained by the low interest rates, the starting point for which is the low riskless rate.

JOEL GREENBLATT: *This may suggest that the risk-free rate should be normalized in some way before being used to assess riskier investments.*

After all, each investment has to compete with others for capital, but this year, due to the low interest rates, the bar for each successively riskier investment has been set lower than at any time in my career.

Not only is the capital market line at a low level today in terms of return, but in addition a number of factors have conspired to flatten it. (This is important, because the slope of the line, or the extent to which expected return rises per unit increase in risk, quantifies the risk premium.) First, investors have fallen over themselves in their effort to get away from low-risk, low-return investments. . . . Second, risky investments have been very rewarding for more than twenty years and did particularly well in 2003. Thus, investors are attracted more (or repelled less) by risky investments than perhaps might otherwise be the case, and require less risk compensation to move to them. . . . Third, investors perceive risk as being quite limited today. . . .

In summary, to use the words of the "quants," risk aversion is down. Somehow, in that alchemy unique to investor psychology, "I wouldn't touch it at any price" had morphed into "looks like a solid investment to me."

"RISK AND RETURN TODAY," OCTOBER 27, 2004

This "richening" process eventually brings on elevated price/earnings ratios, narrow credit spreads, undisciplined investor behavior, heavy use of leverage and strong demand for investment vehicles of all types. Just as these things raise prices and reduce prospective return, they also create a high-risk environment.

~

Risk is incredibly important to investors. It's also ephemeral and unmeasurable. All of this makes it very hard to recognize, especially when emotions are running high. But recognize it we must. In the passage that follows, written in July 2007, I take you through the evaluation process we used at Oaktree to gauge the investment environment and the "risk mood" at the time. In other time periods the specifics might be different, but I hope this example of the thought process will be useful.

Where do we stand today [mid-2007]? In my opinion, there's little mystery. I see low levels of skepticism, fear and risk aversion. Most people are willing to undertake risky investments, often because the promised returns from traditional, safe investments seem so meager. This is true even though the lack of interest in safe investments and the acceptance of risky investments have rendered the slope of the risk/return line quite flat. Risk premiums are generally the skimpiest I've ever seen, but few people are responding by refusing to accept incremental risk. . . .

Markets have tended recently to move up on positive developments and to recover easily from negatives. I see few assets that people are eager to get rid of, and few forced sellers; instead, most assets are strongly bid for. As a result, I'm not aware of any broad markets that I would describe as underpriced or uncrowded. . . .

It is what it is. We've been living in optimistic times. The cycle has been swinging strongly upward. Prices are elevated and risk premiums are slender. Trust has replaced skepticism, and eagerness has replaced reticence. Do you agree or disagree? That's the key question. Answer it first, and the implications for investing become clear.

In the first quarter of this year, significant delinquencies occurred in subprime mortgages. Those directly involved lost a lot of money, and onlookers worried about contagion to other parts of the economy and other markets. In the second quarter, the impact reached CDOs or collateralized debt obligations (structured, tranched investing entities) that had invested in subprime mortgage portfolios, and hedge funds that had bought CDO debt, including two Bear Stearns funds. Those who had to liquidate assets were forced—as usual in tough times—to sell what they could sell, not what they wanted to sell, and not just the offending subprime-linked assets. We began to read about ratings downgrades, margin calls and fire sales, the usual fuel for capital market meltdowns. And in the last few weeks we've begun to see investor reticence on the rise, with new low-grade debt issues repriced, postponed or pulled, leaving bridge loans unrefinanced.

The last four and a half years have been carefree, halcyon times for investors. That doesn't mean it'll stay that way. I'll give Warren Buffett the last word, as I often do: "It's only when the tide goes out that you find out who's been swimming naked." Pollyannas take note: the tide cannot come in forever.

"IT'S ALL GOOD," JULY 16, 2007

I want to point out emphatically that none of the comments in the July 2007 memo, and none of my other warnings, has anything to do with predicting the future. Everything you needed to know in the years leading up to the crash could be discerned through awareness of what was going on in the present.

~

The reality of risk is much less simple and straightforward than the perception. People vastly overestimate their ability to recognize risk and underestimate what it takes to avoid it; thus, they accept risk unknowingly and in so doing contribute to its creation. That's why it's essential to apply uncommon, second-level thinking to the subject.

Risk arises as investor behavior alters the market. Investors bid up assets, accelerating into the present appreciation that otherwise would have occurred in the future, and thus lowering prospective returns. And as their psychology strengthens and they become bolder and less worried, investors cease to demand adequate risk premiums. The ultimate irony lies in the fact that the reward for taking incremental risk shrinks as more people move to take it.

Thus, the market is not a static arena in which investors operate. It is responsive, shaped by investors' own behavior. Their increasing confidence creates more that they should worry about, just as their rising fear and risk aversion combine to widen risk premiums at the same time as they reduce risk. I call this the "perversity of risk."

JOEL GREENBLATT: *A wonderful phrase to keep in mind when working up the courage to buy bargains after severe market drops.*

HOWARD MARKS: *The riskiest things: I'm very happy with the phrase "the perversity of risk." When investors feel risk is high, their actions serve to reduce risk. But when investors believe risk is low, they create dangerous conditions. The market is dynamic rather than static, and it behaves in ways that are counterintuitive.*

"I wouldn't buy that at any price—everyone knows it's too risky." That's something I've heard a lot in my life, and it has given rise to the best investment opportunities I've participated in. . . .

The truth is, the herd is wrong about risk at least as often as it is about return. A broad consensus that something's too hot to handle is almost always wrong. Usually it's the opposite that's true.

I'm firmly convinced that investment risk resides most where it is least perceived, and vice versa:

- When everyone believes something is risky, their unwillingness to buy usually reduces its price to the point where it's not risky at all. Broadly negative opinion can make it the least risky thing, since all optimism has been driven out of its price.
- And, of course, as demonstrated by the experience of Nifty Fifty investors, when everyone believes something embodies no risk, they usually bid it up to the point where it's enormously risky. No risk is feared, and thus no reward for risk bearing—no "risk premium"—is demanded or provided. That can make the thing that's most esteemed the riskiest.

This paradox exists because most investors think quality, as opposed to price, is the determinant of whether something's risky.

JOEL GREENBLATT: *This thought process is pervasive among individual investors. For many, it is the fundamental flaw in their investment process.*

But high quality assets can be risky, and low quality assets can be safe.

CHRISTOPHER DAVIS: *I agree—there are a number of dangers that come from using a term like "quality." First, investors tend to equate "high-quality asset" with "high-quality investment." As a result, there's an incorrect presumption or implication of less risk when taking on "quality" assets. As Marks rightly points out, quite often "high-quality" companies sell for high prices, making them poor investments. Second, "high quality" tends to be a phrase that incorporates a lot of hindsight bias or "halo effect." Usually, people referring to a "high-quality" company are describing a company* *that has performed very well in the past. The future is often quite different. There is a long list of companies that were once described as "high quality" or "built to last" that are no longer around! For this reason, investors should avoid using the word "quality."*

It's just a matter of the price paid for them. . . . Elevated popular opinion, then, isn't just the source of low return potential, but also of high risk.

"EVERYONE KNOWS," APRIL 26, 2007

7

The Most Important Thing Is . . . Controlling Risk

When you boil it all down, it's the investor's job to intelligently bear risk for profit. Doing it well is what separates the best from the rest.

Outstanding investors, in my opinion, are distinguished at least as much for their ability to control risk as they are for generating return.

High absolute return is much more recognizable and titillating than superior risk-adjusted performance. That's why it's high-returning investors who get their pictures in the papers.

CHRISTOPHER DAVIS: *For instance, lottery winners—though no one thinks they are investment geniuses.*

Since it's hard to gauge risk and risk-adjusted performance (even after the fact), and since the importance of managing risk is widely underappreciated, investors rarely gain recognition for having done a great job in this regard. That's especially true in good times.

But in my opinion, great investors are those who take risks that are less than commensurate with the returns they earn. They may produce moderate returns with low risk, or high returns with moderate risk. But achieving high returns with high risk means very little—unless you can do it for many years, in which case that perceived "high risk" either wasn't really high or was exceptionally well managed.

Consider the investors who are recognized for doing a great job, people such as Warren Buffett, Peter Lynch, Bill Miller and Julian Robertson. In general their records are remarkable because of their decades of consistency and absence of disasters, not just their high returns. Each may have had a bad year or two, but in general they dealt as well with risk as with return.

~

Whatever few awards are presented for risk control, they're never given out in good times. The reason is that risk is covert, invisible. Risk—the possibility of loss—is not observable. What is observable is loss, and loss generally happens only when risk collides with negative events.

This is a very important point, so let me give you a couple of analogies to make sure it's clear. Germs cause illness, but germs themselves are not illness. We might say illness is what results when germs take hold. Homes in California may or may not have construction flaws that would make them collapse during earthquakes. We find out only when earthquakes occur.

Likewise, loss is what happens when risk meets adversity. Risk is the potential for loss if things go wrong. As long as things go well, loss does not arise. Risk gives rise to loss only when negative events occur in the environment.

We must remember that when the environment is salutary, that is only one of the environments that could have materialized that day (or that year). (This is Nassim Nicholas Taleb's idea of alternative histories, described in more detail in chapter 16.) The fact that the environment wasn't negative does not mean that it couldn't have been. Thus, the fact that the environment wasn't negative doesn't mean risk control wasn't desirable, even though—as things turned out—it wasn't needed at that time.

The important thing here is the realization that risk may have been present even though loss didn't occur. Therefore, the absence of loss does not necessarily mean the portfolio was safely constructed. So, risk control can be present in good times, but it isn't observable because it's not tested. Ergo, there are no awards. Only a skilled and sophisticated observer can look at a portfolio in good times and divine whether it is a low-risk portfolio or a high-risk portfolio.

In order for a portfolio to make it through tough times, the risk generally has to be well controlled. If the portfolio thrives in good times, however, we can't tell whether risk control was (a) present but not required or (b) lacking. Bottom line: risk control is invisible in good times but still essential, since good times can so easily turn into bad times.

∽

What's the definition of a job well done?

Most observers think the advantage of inefficient markets lies in the fact that a manager can take the same risk as a benchmark, for example, and earn a superior rate of return. Figure 7.1 presents this idea and depicts the manager's "alpha," or value added through skill.

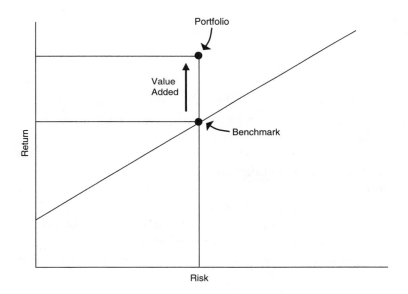

Figure 7.1

This manager has done a good job, but I think this is only half the story—and for me the uninteresting half. An inefficient market can also allow a skilled investor to achieve the same return as the benchmark while taking less risk, and I think this is a great accomplishment (figure 7.2).

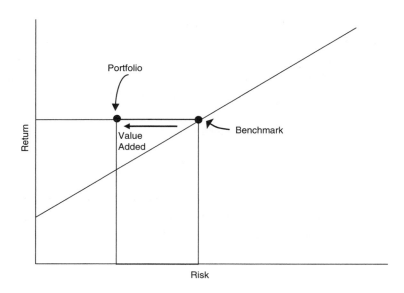

Figure 7.2

Here the manager's value added comes not through higher return at a given risk, but through reduced risk at a given return. This, too, is a good job—maybe even a better one.

Some of this is semantic and depends on how you look at the graphs. But because I think fundamental risk reduction can provide the foundation for an extremely successful investing experience, this concept should receive more attention than it does. How do you enjoy the full gain in up markets while simultaneously being positioned to achieve superior performance in down markets? By capturing the up-market gain while bearing below-market risk . . . no mean feat.

"RETURNS, ABSOLUTE RETURNS AND RISK," JUNE 13, 2006

JOEL GREENBLATT: *Finding such a talent will usually involve assessing the investment process of a manager rather than analyzing returns relative to a benchmark.*

Now we come back to the germs that haven't taken hold, or perhaps the earthquakes that haven't happened. A good builder is able to avoid construction flaws, while a poor builder incorporates construction flaws. When there are no earthquakes, you can't tell the difference.

Likewise, an excellent investor may be one who—rather than reporting higher returns than others—achieves the same return but does so with less risk (or even achieves a slightly lower return with far less risk). Of course, when markets are stable or rising, we don't get to find out how much risk a portfolio entailed. That's what's behind Warren Buffett's observation that other than when the tide goes out, we can't tell which swimmers are clothed and which are naked.

It's an outstanding accomplishment to achieve the same return as the risk bearers and do so with less risk. But most of the time it's a subtle, hidden accomplishment that can be appreciated only through sophisticated judgments.

Since usually there are more good years in the markets than bad years, and since it takes bad years for the value of risk control to become evident in reduced losses, the cost of risk control—in the form of return forgone—can seem excessive. In good years in the market, risk-conscious investors must content themselves with the knowledge that they benefited from its presence in the portfolio, even though it wasn't needed. They're like the prudent homeowners who carry insurance and feel good about having protection in place . . . even when there's no fire.

Controlling the risk in your portfolio is a very important and worthwhile pursuit. The fruits, however, come only in the form of losses that don't happen. Such what-if calculations are difficult in placid times.

PAUL JOHNSON: *This is the ultimate paradox of risk management.*

~

Bearing risk unknowingly can be a huge mistake, but it's what those who buy the securities that are all the rage and most highly esteemed at a particular point in time—to which "nothing bad can possibly happen"—repeatedly do. On the other hand, the intelligent acceptance of recognized risk for profit underlies some of the wisest, most profitable investments—even though (or perhaps due to the fact that) most investors dismiss them as dangerous speculations.

When you boil it all down, it's the investor's job to intelligently bear risk for profit. Doing it well is what separates the best from the rest.

What does it mean to intelligently bear risk for profit? Let's take the example of life insurance. How can life insurance companies—some of the most conservative companies in America—insure people's lives when they know they're *all* going to die?

- It's risk they're aware of. They know everyone's going to die. Thus they factor this reality into their approach.
- It's risk they can analyze. That's why they have doctors assess applicants' health.
- It's risk they can diversify. By ensuring a mix of policyholders by age, gender, occupation and location, they make sure they're not exposed to freak occurrences and widespread losses.
- And it's risk they can be sure they're well paid to bear. They set premiums so they'll make a profit if the policyholders die according to the actuarial tables on average. And if the insurance market is inefficient—for example, if the company can sell a policy to someone likely to die at age eighty at a premium that assumes he'll die at seventy—they'll be better protected against risk and positioned for exceptional profits if things go as expected.

We do exactly the same things in high yield bonds, and in the rest of Oaktree's strategies. We try to be aware of the risks, which is essential given how much our work involves assets that some simplistically call "risky." We employ highly skilled professionals capable of analyzing investments and assessing risk. We diversify our portfolios appropriately. And we invest only when we're convinced the likely return far more than compensates for the risk.

I've said for years that risky assets can make for good investments if they're cheap enough. The essential element is knowing when that's the case. That's it: the intelligent bearing of risk for profit, the best test for which is a record of repeated success over a long period of time.

"RISK," JANUARY 19, 2006

~

While risk control is essential, risk *bearing* is neither wise nor unwise per se. It's inevitably part of most investment strategies and investment niches. It can be done well or poorly, and at the right time or the wrong time. If you have enough skill to be able to move into the more aggressive niches with risk under control, it's the best thing possible. But the potential pitfalls are many, and they must be avoided.

Careful risk controllers know they don't know the future. They know it can include some negative outcomes, but not how bad they might be, or exactly what their probabilities are. Thus, the principal pitfalls come in the inability to know "how bad is bad," and in resulting poor decisions.

> Extreme volatility and loss surface only infrequently. And as time passes without that happening, it appears more and more likely that it'll never happen—that assumptions regarding risk were too conservative. Thus, it becomes tempting to relax rules and increase leverage. And often this is done just before the risk finally rears its head. As Nassim Nicholas Taleb wrote in *Fooled by Randomness*:
>
>> Reality is far more vicious than Russian roulette. First, it delivers the fatal bullet rather infrequently, like a revolver that would have hundreds, even thousands of chambers instead of six. After a few dozen tries, one forgets about the existence of a bullet, under a numbing false sense of security. . . . Second, unlike a well-defined precise game like Russian roulette, where the risks are visible to anyone capable of multiplying and dividing by six, one does not observe the barrel of reality. . . . One is thus capable of unwittingly playing Russian roulette—and calling it by some alternative "low risk" name.
>
> The financial institutions played a high-risk game in 2004–2007 thinking it was a low-risk game, all because their assumptions on losses and volatility were too low. We'd be watching an entirely different picture if only they'd said, "This stuff is potentially risky.

Since home prices have gone up so much and mortgages have been available so easily, there just might be widespread declines in home prices this time. So we're only going to lever up half as much as past performance might suggest."

It's easy to say they should have made more conservative assumptions. But how conservative?

PAUL JOHNSON: *This is the key question when it comes to assessing risk.*

You can't run a business on the basis of worst-case assumptions. You wouldn't be able to do anything. And anyway, a "worst-case assumption" is really a misnomer; there's no such thing, short of a total loss. Now, we know the quants shouldn't have assumed there couldn't be a nationwide decline in home prices. But once you grant that such a decline can happen—for the first time—what extent should you prepare for? Two percent? Ten? Fifty?

The [2008] headlines are full of entities that have seen massive losses, and perhaps meltdowns, because they bought assets using leverage. . . . These investors put on leverage that might have been appropriate with moderate-volatility assets and ran into the greatest volatility ever seen. It's easy to say they made a mistake. But is it reasonable to expect them to have girded for unique events?

If every portfolio was required to be able to withstand declines on the scale we've witnessed this year [2008], it's possible no leverage would ever be used. Is that a reasonable reaction? (In fact, it's possible that no one would ever invest in these asset classes, even on an unlevered basis.)

In all aspects of our lives, we base our decisions on what we think probably will happen. And, in turn, we base that to a great extent on what usually happened in the past. We expect results to be close to the norm (A) most of the time, but we know it's not unusual to see outcomes that are better (B) or worse (C). Although we should bear in mind that, once in a while, a result will be outside the usual range (D), we tend to forget about the potential for outliers. And importantly, as illustrated by recent events, we rarely consider outcomes that have happened only once a century . . . or never (E) (figure 7.3).

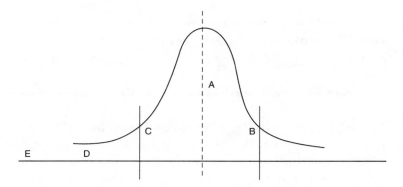

Figure 7.3

Even if we realize that unusual, unlikely things can happen, in order to act we make reasoned decisions and knowingly accept that risk when well paid to do so. Once in a while, a "black swan" will materialize. But if in the future we always said, "We can't do such-and-such, because the outcome could be worse than we've ever seen before," we'd be frozen in inaction.

So in most things, you can't prepare for the worst case. It should suffice to be prepared for once-in-a-generation events. But a generation isn't forever, and there will be times when that standard is exceeded. What do you do about that? I've mused in the past about how much one should devote to preparing for the unlikely disaster. Among other things, the events of 2007–2008 prove there's no easy answer.

"VOLATILITY + LEVERAGE = DYNAMITE," DECEMBER 17, 2008

Especially in view of the vagaries presented previously in this chapter, I want to make clear the important distinction between risk control and risk avoidance. Risk control is the best route to loss avoidance. Risk avoidance, on the other hand, is likely to lead to return avoidance as well. Once in a while I hear someone talk about Oaktree's desire to avoid investment risk and I take great issue.

Clearly, Oaktree doesn't run from risk. We welcome it at the right time, in the right instances, and at the right price.

PAUL JOHNSON: *Marks is clear in his distinction. Risk control is not risk avoidance, and the "right price" is the operative part of his statement.*

We could easily avoid all risk, and so could you. But we'd be assured of avoiding returns above the risk-free rate as well. Will Rogers said, "You've got to go out on a limb sometimes because that's where the fruit is." None of us is in this business to make 4 percent.

So even though the first tenet in Oaktree's investment philosophy stresses "the importance of risk control," this has nothing to do with risk avoidance.

It's by bearing risk when we're well paid to do so—and especially by taking risks toward which others are averse in the extreme— that we strive to add value for our clients. When formulated that way, it's obvious how big a part risk plays in our process.

Rick Funston of Deloitte & Touche said in the article that prompted this memo ("When Corporate Risk Becomes Personal," *Corporate Board Member*, 2005 Special Supplement), "You need comfort that the . . . risks and exposures are understood, appropriately managed, and made more transparent for everyone. . . . This is not risk aversion; it is risk intelligence." That's what Oaktree strives for every day.

"RISK," JANUARY 19, 2006

The road to long-term investment success runs through risk control more than through aggressiveness. Over a full career, most investors' results will be determined more by how many losers they have, and how bad they are, than by the greatness of their winners. Skillful risk control is the mark of the superior investor.

JOEL GREENBLATT: *The math behind the compounding of negative returns helps ensure this outcome (e.g., a 40 percent loss in one year requires a return of 67 percent to fully recover).*

8

The Most Important Thing Is . . . Being Attentive to Cycles

I think it's essential to remember that just about everything is cyclical. There's little I'm certain of, but these things are true: Cycles always prevail eventually. Nothing goes in one direction forever. Trees don't grow to the sky. Few things go to zero. And there's little that's as dangerous for investor health as insistence on extrapolating today's events into the future.

The more time I spend in the world of investing, the more I appreciate the underlying cyclicality of things. In November 2001 I devoted an entire memo to the subject. I titled it "You Can't Predict. You Can Prepare," borrowing the advertising tagline of MassMutual Life Insurance Company because I agree wholeheartedly with their theme: we never know what lies ahead, but we can prepare for the possibilities and reduce their sting.

In investing, as in life, there are very few sure things. Values can evaporate, estimates can be wrong, circumstances can change and "sure things" can fail. However, there are two concepts we can hold to with confidence:

- *Rule number one:* most things will prove to be cyclical.
- *Rule number two:* some of the greatest opportunities for gain and loss come when other people forget rule number one.

Very few things move in a straight line. There's progress and then there's deterioration. Things go well for a while and then poorly. Progress may be swift and then slow down. Deterioration may creep up gradually and then turn climactic. But the underlying principle is that things will wax and wane, grow and decline. The same is true for economies, markets and companies: they rise and fall.

The basic reason for the cyclicality in our world is the involvement of humans. Mechanical things can go in a straight line. Time moves ahead continuously. So can a machine when it's adequately powered. But processes in fields like history and economics involve people, and when people are involved, the results are variable and cyclical. The main reason for this, I think, is that people are emotional and inconsistent, not steady and clinical.

Objective factors do play a large part in cycles, of course—factors such as quantitative relationships, world events, environmental changes, technological developments and corporate decisions. But it's the application of psychology to these things that causes investors to overreact or underreact, and thus determines the amplitude of the cyclical fluctuations.

When people feel good about the way things are going and optimistic about the future, their behavior is strongly impacted. They spend more and save less. They borrow to increase their enjoyment or their profit potential, even though doing so makes their financial position more precarious (of course, concepts like precariousness are forgotten in optimistic times). And they become willing to pay more for current value or a piece of the future.

All of these things are capable of reversing in a second; one of my favorite cartoons features a TV commentator saying, "Everything that was good for the market yesterday is no good for it today." The extremes of cycles result largely from people's emotions and foibles, nonobjectivity and inconsistency.

Cycles are self-correcting, and their reversal is not necessarily dependent on exogenous events. They reverse (rather than going on forever) because trends create the reasons for their own reversal. Thus, I like to say success carries within itself the seeds of failure, and failure the seeds of success.

"YOU CAN'T PREDICT. YOU CAN PREPARE," NOVEMBER 20, 2001

~

The credit cycle deserves a very special mention for its inevitability, extreme volatility and ability to create opportunities for investors attuned to it. Of all the cycles, it's my favorite.

The longer I'm involved in investing, the more impressed I am by the power of the credit cycle. It takes only a small fluctuation in the economy to produce a large fluctuation in the availability of credit, with great impact on asset prices and back on the economy itself.

The process is simple:

- The economy moves into a period of prosperity.
- Providers of capital thrive, increasing their capital base.
- Because bad news is scarce, the risks entailed in lending and investing seem to have shrunk.
- Risk averseness disappears.
- Financial institutions move to expand their businesses—that is, to provide more capital.
- They compete for market share by lowering demanded returns (e.g., cutting interest rates), lowering credit standards, providing more capital for a given transaction and easing covenants.

At the extreme, providers of capital finance borrowers and projects that aren't worthy of being financed. As *The Economist* said earlier this year, "the worst loans are made at the best of times."

PAUL JOHNSON: *This insight is hard to fully comprehend until one has been hurt by not following its sage advice! Although students nod their heads in agreement when the topic is discussed in class, they are the investors and bankers that will undoubtedly repeat this mistake in the future.*

This leads to capital destruction—that is, to investment of capital in projects where the cost of capital exceeds the return *on* capital, and eventually to cases where there is no return *of* capital.

When this point is reached, the up-leg described above—the rising part of the cycle—is reversed.

- Losses cause lenders to become discouraged and shy away.
- Risk averseness rises, and along with it, interest rates, credit restrictions and covenant requirements.
- Less capital is made available—and at the trough of the cycle, only to the most qualified of borrowers, if anyone.
- Companies become starved for capital. Borrowers are unable to roll over their debts, leading to defaults and bankruptcies.
- This process contributes to and reinforces the economic contraction.

Of course, at the extreme the process is ready to be reversed again. Because the competition to make loans or investments is low, high returns can be demanded along with high creditworthiness.

CHRISTOPHER DAVIS: *Again, you get higher return and lower risk.*

Contrarians who commit capital at this point have a shot at high returns, and those tempting potential returns begin to draw in capital. In this way, a recovery begins to be fueled.

I stated earlier that cycles are self-correcting. The credit cycle corrects itself through the processes described above, and it represents one of the factors driving the fluctuations of the economic cycle. Prosperity brings expanded lending, which leads to unwise lending, which produces large losses, which makes lenders stop lending, which ends prosperity, and on and on.

. . . Look around the next time there's a crisis; you'll probably find a lender. Overpermissive providers of capital frequently aid and abet financial bubbles. There have been numerous recent examples where loose credit contributed to booms that were followed by famous collapses: real estate in 1989–1992; emerging markets in 1994–1998; Long-Term Capital Management in 1998; the movie exhibition industry in 1999–2000; venture capital funds and telecommunications companies in 2000–2001. In each case, lenders and investors provided too much cheap money and the result was overexpansion and dramatic losses. In *Field of Dreams*, Kevin

Costner was told, "If you build it, they will come." In the financial world, if you offer cheap money, they will borrow, buy and build—often without discipline, and with very negative consequences.

"YOU CAN'T PREDICT. YOU CAN PREPARE,"

NOVEMBER 20, 2001

PAUL JOHNSON: *I continue to be impressed, throughout the book, with how decade-old memos read as fresh as recently written ones. This memo is a prime example. Marks's use of his old memos is particularly effective in showing that history repeats or, at least, that man has a tendency to repeat history.*

Please note that this memo, written almost ten years ago, perfectly describes the process through which the 2007–2008 financial crisis arose. It wasn't predictive ability that enabled me to write it—just familiarity with a never-ending underlying cycle.

JOEL GREENBLATT: *Understanding that cycles are eventually self-correcting is one way to maintain some optimism when bargain hunting after large market drops.*

Cycles will never stop occurring. If there were such a thing as a completely efficient market, and if people really made decisions in a calculating and unemotional manner, perhaps cycles (or at least their extremes) would be banished. But that'll never be the case.

Economies will wax and wane as consumers spend more or less, responding emotionally to economic factors or exogenous events, geopolitical or naturally occurring. Companies will anticipate a rosy future during the up cycle and thus overexpand facilities and inventories; these will become burdensome when the economy turns down. Providers of capital will be too generous when the economy's doing well, abetting overexpansion with cheap money, and then they'll pull the reins too tight when things cease to look as good.

//

SETH KLARMAN: *Indeed, this is an essential virtue of capitalism. Oversupply of a good leads to a price decline and lower profits. Suppliers of that good stop expanding and contract if they can. A market-based system will respond in ways a centrally planned economy cannot, leading to more optimal use of society's resources.*

\\

Investors will overvalue companies when they're doing well and undervalue them when things get difficult.

And yet, every decade or so, people decide cyclicality is over. They think either the good times will roll on without end or the negative trends can't be arrested. At such times they talk about "virtuous cycles" or "vicious cycles"— self-feeding developments that will go on forever in one direction or the other.

Case in point: On November 15, 1996, *The Wall Street Journal* reported on a growing consensus: "From boardrooms to living rooms and from government offices to trading floors, a new consensus is emerging: The big, bad business cycle has been tamed." Does anyone remember a steady, non-cyclical economic environment in the years since then? What would explain the emerging crisis of 1998, the recession of 2002, and the financial crisis—and worst recession since World War II—of 2008?

This belief that cyclicality has been ended exemplifies a way of thinking based on the dangerous premise that "this time it's different." These four words should strike fear—and perhaps suggest an opportunity for profit— for anyone who understands the past and knows it repeats. Thus, it's essential that you be able to recognize this form of error when it arises.

One of my favorite books is a little volume titled *Oh Yeah?*, a 1932 compilation of pre-Depression wisdom from businessmen and political leaders. It seems that even then, pundits were predicting a cycle-free economy:

- There will be no interruption of our present prosperity. (Myron E. Forbes, President, Pierce Arrow Motor Car Co., January 1, 1928)
- I cannot help but raise a dissenting voice to the statements that . . . prosperity in this country must necessarily diminish and recede in the future. (E.H.H. Simmons, President, New York Stock Exchange, January 12, 1928)
- We are only at the beginning of a period that will go down in history as the golden age. (Irving T. Bush, President, Bush Terminal Co., November 15, 1928)

- The fundamental business of the country . . . is on a sound and prosperous basis. (President Herbert Hoover, October 25, 1929)

> Every once in a while, an up- or down-leg goes on for a long time and/or to a great extreme and people start to say "this time it's different." They cite the changes in geopolitics, institutions, technology or behavior that have rendered the "old rules" obsolete. They make investment decisions that extrapolate the recent trend. And then it turns out that the old rules do still apply, and the cycle resumes. In the end, trees don't grow to the sky, and few things go to zero. Rather, most phenomena turn out to be cyclical.
>
> "YOU CAN'T PREDICT. YOU CAN PREPARE," NOVEMBER 20, 2001

> We conclude that most of the time, the future will look a lot like the past, with both up cycles and down cycles. There is a right time to argue that things will be better, and that's when the market is on its backside and everyone else is selling things at giveaway prices. It's dangerous when the market's at record levels to reach for a positive rationalization that has never held true in the past. But it's been done before, and it'll be done again.
>
> "WILL IT BE DIFFERENT THIS TIME?" NOVEMBER 25, 1996

Ignoring cycles and extrapolating trends is one of the most dangerous things an investor can do. People often act as if companies that are doing well will do well forever, and investments that are outperforming will outperform forever, and vice versa. Instead, it's the opposite that's more likely to be true.

HOWARD MARKS: *The riskiest things: When things are going well, extrapolation introduces great risk. Whether it's company profitability, capital availability, price gains, or market liquidity, things that inevitably are bound to regress toward the mean are often counted on to improve forever.*

The first time rookie investors see this phenomenon occur, it's understandable that they might accept that something that's never happened before—the cessation of cycles— could happen. But the second time or the third time, those investors, now experienced, should realize it's never going to happen, and turn that realization to their advantage.

The next time you're approached with a deal predicated on cycles having ceased to occur, remember that invariably that's a losing bet.

9
The Most Important Thing Is . . .
Awareness of the Pendulum

When things are going well and prices are high, investors rush to buy, forgetting all prudence. Then, when
there's chaos all around and assets are on the bargain
counter, they lose all willingness to bear risk and rush to
sell. And it will ever be so.

The second investor memo I ever wrote, back in 1991, was devoted almost
entirely to a subject that I have come to think about more and more over the
years: the pendulum-like oscillation of investor attitudes and behavior.

PAUL JOHNSON: *Chapter 9 is essentially an extension of the three
earlier chapters on risk and offers additional insight into how to
analyze the current risk temperature in the markets.*

The mood swings of the securities markets resemble the movement of a pendulum. Although the midpoint of its arc best describes
the location of the pendulum "on average," it actually spends very
little of its time there. Instead, it is almost always swinging toward
or away from the extremes of its arc. But whenever the pendulum
is near either extreme, it is inevitable that it will move back toward the midpoint sooner or later. In fact, it is the movement toward
an extreme itself that supplies the energy for the swing back.

Investment markets follow a pendulum-like swing:

- between euphoria and depression,
- between celebrating positive developments and obsessing over negatives, and thus
- between overpriced and underpriced.

This oscillation is one of the most dependable features of the investment world, and investor psychology seems to spend much more time at the extremes than it does at a "happy medium."

"FIRST QUARTER PERFORMANCE," APRIL 11, 1991

Thirteen years later I revisited the subject of the pendulum at length in another memo. In it I observed that in addition to the elements mentioned earlier, the pendulum also swings with regard to greed versus fear; willingness to view things through an optimistic or a pessimistic lens; faith in developments that are on-the-come; credulousness versus skepticism; and risk tolerance versus risk aversion.

The swing in the last of these—attitudes toward risk—is a common thread that runs through many of the market's fluctuations.

Risk aversion is *the* essential ingredient in a rational market, as I said before, and the position of the pendulum with regard to it is particularly important. Improper amounts of risk aversion are key contributors to the market excesses of bubble and crash. It's an oversimplification—but not a grievous one—to say the inevitable hallmark of bubbles is a dearth of risk aversion. In crashes, on the other hand, investors fear too much. Excessive risk aversion keeps them from buying even when no optimism—only pessimism—is embodied in prices and valuations are absurdly low.

In my opinion, the greed/fear cycle is caused by changing attitudes toward risk. When greed is prevalent, it means investors feel a high level of comfort with risk and the idea of bearing it in the interest of profit. Conversely, widespread fear indicates a high level of aversion to risk. The academics consider investors' attitude toward risk a constant, but certainly it fluctuates greatly.

Finance theory is heavily dependent on the assumption that investors are risk-averse. That is, they "disprefer" risk and must be induced—bribed—to bear it, with higher expected returns.

Reaping dependably high returns from risky investments is an oxymoron. But there are times when this caveat is ignored—when people get too comfortable with risk and thus when prices of securities incorporate a premium for bearing risk that is inadequate to compensate for the risk that's present. . . .

//

PAUL JOHNSON: *Marks links risk and security prices/valuation directly, something that is not done in general finance theory but is exceedingly important for investors to understand.*

\\

When investors in general are too risk-tolerant, security prices can embody more risk than they do return. When investors are too risk-averse, prices can offer more return than risk.

"THE HAPPY MEDIUM," JULY 21, 2004

The pendulum swing regarding attitudes toward risk is one of the most powerful of all. In fact, I've recently boiled down the main risks in investing to two: the risk of losing money and the risk of missing opportunity. It's possible to largely eliminate either one, but not both. In an ideal world, investors would balance these two concerns. But from time to time, at the extremes of the pendulum's swing, one or the other predominates. For example:

- In 2005, 2006 and early 2007, with things going so swimmingly and the capital markets wide open, few people imagined that losses could lie ahead. Many believed risk had been banished. Their only worry was that they might miss an opportunity; if Wall Street came out with a new financial miracle and other investors bought and they didn't—and if the miracle worked—they might look unprogressive and lose ground. Since they weren't concerned about losing money, they didn't insist on low purchase prices, adequate risk premiums or investor protection. In short, they behaved too aggressively.
- Then in late 2007 and 2008, with the credit crisis in full flower, people began to fear a complete meltdown of the world financial system. No one worried about missing opportunity; the pendulum had swung to the point

where people worried only about losing money. Thus, they ran from anything with a scintilla of risk—regardless of the potential return—and to the safety of government securities with yields near zero. At this point, then, investors feared too much, sold too eagerly and positioned their portfolios too defensively.

SETH KLARMAN: *Paul Isaac has called this "return-free risk."*

PAUL JOHNSON: *These two bullets provide an excellent recap of the many mistakes investors made in the years leading up to the 2008 financial crisis.*

Thus, the last several years have provided an unusually clear opportunity to witness the swing of the pendulum . . . and how consistently most people do the wrong thing at the wrong time. When things are going well and prices are high, investors rush to buy, forgetting all prudence. Then, when there's chaos all around and assets are on the bargain counter, they lose all willingness to bear risk and rush to sell. And it will ever be so.

Very early in my career, a veteran investor told me about the three stages of a bull market. Now I'll share them with you.

- The first, when a few forward-looking people begin to believe things will get better
- The second, when most investors realize improvement is actually taking place
- The third, when everyone concludes things will get better forever

Why would anyone waste time trying for a better description? This one says it all. It's essential that we grasp its significance.

The market has a mind of its own, and it's changes in valuation parameters, caused primarily by changes in investor psychology (not changes in fundamentals), that account for most short-term changes in security prices. This psychology, too, moves like a pendulum.

Stocks are cheapest when everything looks grim.

PAUL JOHNSON: *This short comment furthers Marks's point about the financial crisis. These few words capture the challenges of successful investing. It is hard for the average investor to commit capital to a new investment when the outlook is gloomy. Yet it is precisely in these moments that potential returns are at their highest.*

The depressing outlook keeps them there, and only a few astute and daring bargain hunters are willing to take new positions. Maybe their buying attracts some attention, or maybe the outlook turns a little less depressing, but for one reason or another, the market starts moving up.

After a while, the outlook seems a little less poor. People begin to appreciate that improvement is taking place, and it requires less imagination to be a buyer. Of course, with the economy and market off the critical list, they pay prices that are more reflective of stocks' fair values.

And eventually, giddiness sets in. Cheered by the improvement in economic and corporate results, people become willing to extrapolate it. The masses become excited (and envious) about the profits made by investors who were early, and they want in. And they ignore the cyclical nature of things and conclude that the gains will go on forever. That's why I love the old adage "What the wise man does in the beginning, the fool does in the end." Most important, in the late stages of the great bull markets, people become willing to pay prices for stocks that assume the good times will go on ad infinitum.

"YOU CAN'T PREDICT. YOU CAN PREPARE," NOVEMBER 20, 2001

HOWARD MARKS: *The riskiest things: The ultimate danger zone is reached when investors are in agreement that things can only get better forever. That makes no sense, but most people fall for it. It's what creates bubbles—just as the opposite produces crashes.*

Thirty-five years after I first learned about the stages of a bull market, after the weaknesses of subprime mortgages (and their holders) had been exposed and as people were worrying about contagion to a global crisis, I came up with the flip side, the three stages of a bear market:

- The first, when just a few thoughtful investors recognize that, despite the prevailing bullishness, things won't always be rosy
- The second, when most investors recognize things are deteriorating
- The third, when everyone's convinced things can only get worse

Certainly we're well into the second of these three stages. There's been lots of bad news and write-offs. More and more people recognize the dangers inherent in things like innovation, leverage, derivatives, counterparty risk and mark-to-market accounting. And increasingly the problems seem insolvable.

One of these days, though, we'll reach the third stage, and the herd will give up on there being a solution. And unless the financial world really does end, we're likely to encounter the investment opportunities of a lifetime. Major bottoms occur when everyone forgets that the tide also comes in. Those are the times we live for.

"THE TIDE GOES OUT," MARCH 18, 2008

Just six months after those words were written, the progression had gone all the way to the third stage. A full meltdown of the world financial system was considered possible; in fact, the first steps—the bankruptcy of Lehman Brothers and the absorption or rescue of Bear Stearns, Merrill Lynch, AIG, Fannie Mae, Freddie Mac, Wachovia and WaMu—had taken place. Since this was the biggest crisis ever, investors bought into the third stage, during which "everyone's convinced things can only get worse," more than ever before. Thus, in many asset classes, the things determined by the pendulum's swing—the price declines in 2008, the resultant investment opportunities at the nadir, and the gains in 2009—were the greatest I've ever seen.

The significance of all this is the opportunity it offers to those who recognize what is happening and see the implications. At one extreme of the pendulum—the darkest of times—it takes analytical ability, objectivity, resolve, even imagination, to think things will ever get better. The few people who possess those qualities can make unusual profits with low risk. But at the other extreme, when everyone assumes and prices in the impossible—improvement forever—the stage is set for painful losses.

It all goes together. None of these is an isolated event or a chance occurrence. Rather, they're all elements in a recurring pattern that can be understood and profited from.

~

The oscillation of the investor pendulum is very similar in nature to the up-and-down fluctuation of economic and market cycles described in chapter 8. For some reason I find myself making a distinction between the two and speaking of them in different terms, but they're both highly important, and the key lessons are the same. With the benefit of almost twenty years' experience since writing that first memo about the pendulum in 1991, I'll rephrase its key observations:

- In theory with regard to polarities such as fear and greed, the pendulum should reside mostly at a midpoint between the extremes. But it doesn't for long.

> **JOEL GREENBLATT:** *This means markets will always create opportunities, whether now or later. In markets with few opportunities, it's important to be patient. Value opportunities will eventually present themselves, usually after no more than a year or two.*

- Primarily because of the workings of investor psychology, it's usually swinging toward or back from one extreme or the other.
- The pendulum cannot continue to swing toward an extreme, or reside at an extreme, forever (although when it's positioned at its greatest extreme, people increasingly describe that as having become a permanent condition).
- Like a pendulum, the swing of investor psychology toward an extreme causes energy to build up that eventually will contribute to the swing back in the other direction. Sometimes, the pent-up energy is itself the cause of the swing back—that is, the pendulum's swing toward an extreme corrects of its very weight.

- The swing back from the extreme is usually more rapid—and thus takes much less time—than the swing to the extreme. (Or as my partner Sheldon Stone likes to say, "The air goes out of the balloon much faster than it went in.")

The occurrence of this pendulum-like pattern in most market phenomena is extremely dependable. But just like the oscillation of cycles, we never know:

- how far the pendulum will swing in its arc,
- what might cause the swing to stop and turn back,
- when this reversal will occur, or
- how far it will then swing in the opposite direction.

> For a bullish phase . . . to hold sway, the environment has to be characterized by greed, optimism, exuberance, confidence, credulity, daring, risk tolerance and aggressiveness. But these traits will not govern a market forever. Eventually they will give way to fear, pessimism, prudence, uncertainty, skepticism, caution, risk aversion and reticence. . . . Busts are the product of booms, and I'm convinced it's usually more correct to attribute a bust to the excesses of the preceding boom than to the specific event that sets off the correction.
>
> "NOW WHAT?" JANUARY 10, 2008

There are a few things of which we can be sure, and this is one: Extreme market behavior will reverse. Those who believe that the pendulum will move in one direction forever—or reside at an extreme forever—eventually will lose huge sums. Those who understand the pendulum's behavior can benefit enormously.

10

The Most Important Thing Is . . . Combating Negative Influences

---

The desire for more, the fear of missing out, the tendency to compare against others, the influence of the crowd and the dream of the sure thing—these factors are near universal. Thus they have a profound collective impact on most investors and most markets. The result is mistakes, and those mistakes are frequent, widespread and recurring.

PAUL JOHNSON: *This is an excellent description of the emotional pressure most investors feel when confronted with the power of a bull market—and as Marks points out, few of us are immune to these forces.*

Inefficiencies—mispricings, misperceptions, mistakes that other people make—provide potential opportunities for superior performance. Exploiting them is, in fact, the *only* road to consistent outperformance. To distinguish yourself from the others, you need to be on the right side of those mistakes.

~

Why do mistakes occur? Because investing is an action undertaken by human beings, most of whom are at the mercy of their psyches and emotions.

CHRISTOPHER DAVIS: *And not only their psyches and emotions— perverse incentives can influence institutional investors' decision making in negative ways.*

Many people possess the intellect needed to analyze data, but far fewer are able to look more deeply into things and withstand the powerful influence of psychology. To say this another way, many people will reach similar cognitive conclusions from their analysis, but what they do with those conclusions varies all over the lot because psychology influences them differently. The biggest investing errors come not from factors that are informational or analytical, but from those that are psychological. Investor psychology includes many separate elements, which we will look at in this chapter, but the key thing to remember is that they consistently lead to incorrect decisions. Much of this falls under the heading of "human nature."

HOWARD MARKS: *Emotion and ego: Psychological influences have great power over investors. Most succumb, permitting investor psychology to determine the swings of the market. When those forces push markets to extremes of bubble or crash, they create opportunities for superior investors to augment their results by refusing to hold at the highs and by insisting on buying at the lows. Resisting the inimical forces is an absolute requirement.*

The first emotion that serves to undermine investors' efforts is the desire for money, especially as it morphs into *greed*.

Most people invest to make money. (Some participate as an intellectual exercise or because it's a good field in which to vent their competitiveness, but even they keep score in terms of money. Money may not be everyone's goal for its own sake, but it is everyone's unit of account. People who don't care about money generally don't go into investing.)

There's nothing wrong with trying to make money. Indeed, the desire for gain is one of the most important elements in the workings of the market and the overall economy. The danger comes when it moves on further to greed, which *Merriam-Webster's* defines as an "inordinate or all-consuming and usually reprehensible acquisitiveness especially for wealth or gain."

Greed is an extremely powerful force. It's strong enough to overcome common sense, risk aversion, prudence, caution, logic, memory of painful past lessons, resolve, trepidation and all the other elements that might otherwise keep investors out of trouble. Instead, from time to time greed drives investors to throw in their lot with the crowd in pursuit of profit, and eventually they pay the price.

The combination of greed and optimism repeatedly leads people to pursue strategies they hope will produce high returns without high risk; pay elevated prices for securities that are in vogue; and hold things after they have become highly priced in the hope there's still some appreciation left. Afterwards, hindsight shows everyone what went wrong: that expectations were unrealistic and risks were ignored.

"HINDSIGHT FIRST, PLEASE (OR, WHAT WERE THEY THINKING?),"
OCTOBER 17, 2005

The counterpart of greed is *fear*—the second psychological factor we must consider. In the investment world the term doesn't mean logical, sensible risk aversion. Rather, *fear*—like greed—connotes excess. Fear, then, is more like panic. Fear is overdone concern that prevents investors from taking constructive action when they should.

Many times over the course of my career, I've been amazed by how easy it is for people to engage in *willing suspension of disbelief.* Thus, the third factor I want to discuss is people's tendency to dismiss logic, history and time-honored norms. This tendency makes people accept unlikely propositions that have the potential to make them rich . . . if only they held water. Charlie Munger gave me a great quotation on this subject, from Demosthenes: "Nothing is easier than self-deceit. For what each man wishes, that he also believes to be true." The belief that some fundamental limiter is no longer valid—and thus historic notions of fair value no longer matter—is invariably at the core of every bubble and consequent crash.

In fiction, willing suspension of disbelief adds to our enjoyment. When we watch *Peter Pan*, we don't want to hear the person sitting next to us say, "I can see the wires" (even though we know they're there). While we know boys can't fly, we don't care; we're just there for fun.

But our purpose in investing is serious, not fun, and we must constantly be on the lookout for things that can't work in real life. In short, the process of investing requires a strong dose of disbelief. . . . Inadequate skepticism contributes to investment losses. Time and time again, the postmortems of financial debacles include two classic phrases: "It was too good to be true" and "What were they thinking?"

"HINDSIGHT FIRST, PLEASE (OR, WHAT WERE THEY THINKING?),"
OCTOBER 17, 2005

What makes investors fall for these delusions? The answer often lies in the ease with which—often in service to greed—they dismiss or ignore the lessons of the past. "Extreme brevity of the financial memory," to use John Kenneth Galbraith's wonderful phrase, keeps market participants from recognizing the recurring nature of these patterns, and thus their inevitability:

When the same or closely similar circumstances occur again, sometimes in only a few years, they are hailed by a new, often youthful, and always supremely self-confident generation as a brilliantly innovative discovery in the financial and larger economic world. There can be few fields of human endeavor in which history counts for so little as in the world of finance. Past experience, to the extent that it is part of memory at all, is dismissed as the primitive refuge of those who do not have the insight to appreciate the incredible wonders of the present. (John Kenneth Galbraith, *A Short History of Financial Euphoria* [New York: Viking, 1990])

///

JOEL GREENBLATT: *Many of the mistakes I have made are the same ones that I had made before; they just look a little different each time—the same mistake slightly disguised.*

\\\

The infallible investment that people come to believe can produce high returns without risk—the sure thing or free lunch—is well worth further discussion.

When a market, an individual or an investment technique produces impressive returns for a while, it generally attracts excessive (and unquestioning) devotion. I call this solution du jour the "silver bullet."

Investors are always looking for it. Call it the holy grail or the free lunch, but everyone wants a ticket to riches without risk. Few people question whether it can exist or why it should be available to them. At the bottom line, hope springs eternal.

But the silver bullet doesn't exist. No strategy can produce high rates of return without risk. And nobody has all the answers; we're all just human. Markets are highly dynamic, and, among other things, they function over time to take away the opportunity for unusual profits. Unskeptical belief that the silver bullet is at hand eventually leads to capital punishment.

"THE REALIST'S CREED," MAY 31, 2002

What makes for belief in silver bullets? First, there's usually a germ of truth.

JOEL GREENBLATT: *Remember, if theories (like rumors) didn't have this germ of truth, no one would have believed them in the first place.*

It's spun into an intelligent-sounding theory, and adherents get on their soapboxes to convince others. Then it produces profits for a while, whether because there's merit in it or just because buying on the part of new converts lifts the price of the subject asset. Eventually, the appearance that (a) there's a path to sure wealth and (b) it's working turns it into a mania. As Warren Buffett told Congress on June 2, 2010, "Rising prices are a narcotic that affects the reasoning power up and down the line." But after the fact—after it has popped—a mania is called a bubble.

The fourth psychological contributor to investor error is the *tendency to conform to the view of the herd* rather than resist—even when the herd's view is clearly cockeyed. In *How Markets Fail*, John Cassidy describes classic psychology experiments conducted by Swarthmore's Solomon Asch in the 1950s. Asch asked groups of subjects to make judgments about visual exhibits, but all but one of the "subjects" in each group were shills working for him. The shills intentionally said the wrong thing, with dramatic impact on the one real subject. Cassidy explains, "This setup placed the genuine subject in an awkward spot: [As Asch put it,] 'Upon him we have brought to bear two opposed forces: the evidence of his senses and the unanimous opinion of a group of his peers.'"

A high percentage of the real subjects ignored what they saw and sided with the other group members, even though they were obviously in the wrong. This indicates the influence of the crowd and thus suggests reservations about the validity of consensus decisions.

"Like the participants in Solomon Asch's visual experiments in the 1950s," Cassidy writes, "many people who don't share the consensus view of the market start to feel left out. Eventually it reaches a stage where it appears the really crazy people are those not in the market."

Time and time again, the combination of pressure to conform and the desire to get rich causes people to drop their independence and skepticism, overcome their innate risk aversion and believe things that don't make sense. It happens so regularly that there must be something dependable at work, not a random influence.

The fifth psychological influence is *envy*. However negative the force of greed might be, always spurring people to strive for more and more, the impact is even stronger when they compare themselves to others. This is one of the most harmful aspects of what we call human nature.

People who might be perfectly happy with their lot in isolation become miserable when they see others do better. In the world of investing, most people find it terribly hard to sit by and watch while others make more money than they do.

///

HOWARD MARKS: *Emotion and ego: A lot of the drive in investing is competitive. High returns can be unsatisfying if others do better, while low returns are often enough if others do worse. The tendency to compare results is one of the most invidious. The emphasis on relative returns over absolute returns shows how psychology can distort the process.*

I know of a nonprofit institution whose endowment earned 16 percent a year from June 1994 to June 1999, but since its peers averaged 23 percent, the people involved with the endowment were dejected.

SETH KLARMAN: *Even the best investors judge themselves on the basis of return. It would be hard to evaluate yourself on risk, since risk cannot be measured. Apparently, the risk-averse managers of this endowment were disappointed with their relative returns even though their risk-adjusted performance was likely excellent, as borne out by their performance over the following three years. This highlights just how hard it is to maintain conviction over the long run when short-term performance is considered poor.*

Without growth stocks, technology stocks, buyouts and venture capital, the endowment was entirely out of step for half a decade. But then the tech stocks collapsed, and from June 2000 to June 2003 the institution earned 3 percent a year while most endowments suffered losses. The stakeholders were thrilled.

There's something wrong with this picture. How can people be unhappy making 16 percent a year and happy making 3 percent? The answer lies in the tendency to compare ourselves to others and the deleterious impact this can have on what should be a constructive, analytical process.

JOEL GREENBLATT: *This is incredibly important. Most institutional and individual investors benchmark their returns, and therefore most end up chasing the crowd: accent on the wrong sylLABle.*

The sixth key influence is *ego*. It can be enormously challenging to remain objective and calculating in the face of facts like these:

- Investment results are evaluated and compared in the short run.
- Incorrect, even imprudent, decisions to bear increased risk generally lead to the best returns in good times (and most times are good times).
- The best returns bring the greatest ego rewards. When things go right, it's fun to feel smart and have others agree.

HOWARD MARKS: *Emotion and ego: Investing—especially poor investing—is a world full of ego. Since risk bearing is rewarded in rising markets, ego can make investors behave aggressively in order*

to stand out through the achievement of lofty results. But the best
investors I know seek stellar risk-adjusted returns . . . not celebrity.
In my view, the road to investment success is usually marked by
humility, not ego.

In contrast, thoughtful investors can toil in obscurity, achieving solid gains in the good years and losing less than others in the bad. They avoid sharing in the riskiest behavior because they're so aware of how much they don't know and because they have their egos in check. This, in my opinion, is the greatest formula for long-term wealth creation—but it doesn't provide much ego gratification in the short run. It's just not that glamorous to follow a path that emphasizes humility, prudence and risk control. Of course, investing shouldn't be about glamour, but often it is.

Finally, I want to mention a phenomenon I call *capitulation*, a regular feature of investor behavior late in cycles. Investors hold to their convictions as long as they can, but when the economic and psychological pressures become irresistible, they surrender and jump on the bandwagon.

In general, people who go into the investment business are intelligent, educated, informed and numerate. They master the nuances of business and economics and understand complex theories. Many are able to reach reasonable conclusions about value and prospects.

But then psychology and crowd influences move in. Much of the time, assets are overpriced and appreciating further, or underpriced and still cheapening. Eventually these trends have a corrosive effect on investors' psyches, conviction and resolve. The stocks you rejected are making money for others, the ones you chose to buy are lower every day, and concepts you dismissed as unsafe or unwise—hot new issues, high-priced tech stocks without earnings, highly levered mortgage derivatives—are described daily as delivering for others.

As an overpriced stock goes even higher or an underpriced stock continues to cheapen, it should get easier to do the right thing: sell the former and buy the latter. But it doesn't. The tendency toward self-doubt combines with news of other people's successes to form a powerful force that makes investors do the wrong thing, and it gains additional strength as these trends go on longer. It's one more influence that must be fought.

HOWARD MARKS: *Fear of looking wrong: Assets become over-priced because of investor behavior that overrates their merit and* *carries them aloft. This process shouldn't be expected to come to a halt when the price has risen to the "right" level or when you've sold it because you feel it's priced too high. Usually, the freight train rumbles on quite a bit further, and price judgments are much more likely to look wrong at first than right. Although understandable, this can be very hard to live with.*

The desire for more, the fear of missing out, the tendency to compare against others, the influence of the crowd and the dream of the sure thing—these factors are near universal. Thus they have a profound collective impact on most investors and most markets. This is especially true at the market extremes. The result is mistakes—frequent, widespread, recurring, expensive mistakes.

HOWARD MARKS: *Emotion and Ego: Most Swings toward the extreme of bubble and crazh are based on a seed of truth, usually subjected to reasonable analysis . . . at least at first. But psychological forces cause conclusions to incorporate error, and markets to go too far in incorporating those conclusions. The gravest market losses have their genesis in psychological errors, not analytical miscues.*

Does all this strike you as just so much theorizing, something that couldn't possibly apply to you? I sincerely hope you're right. But just in case you doubt that rational people could succumb to the damaging forces of emotion, let me remind you of two little words: tech bubble. Earlier I mentioned that crazy time as evidence of what happens when investors disregard the need for a reasonable relationship between value and price. What is it that causes them to abandon common sense? Some of the same emotions we have been talking about here: greed, fear, envy, self-deceit, ego. Let's review the scenario and watch psychology at work.

The 1990s were a very strong period for stocks. There were bad days and months, of course, and traumas such as a big jump in interest rates in 1994, but Standard & Poor's 500 stock index showed a gain every year from 1991 through 1999 inclusive, and its return averaged 20.8 percent per year.

Those results were enough to put investors in an optimistic mood and render them receptive to bullish stories.

Growth stocks performed a bit better than value stocks in the early part of the decade—perhaps as a rebound from value's outperformance in the 1980s. This, too, increased investors' willingness to highly value companies' growth potential.

Investors became enthralled by technological innovation. Developments such as broadband, the Internet and e-commerce seemed likely to change the world, and tech and telecom entrepreneurs were lionized.

Tech stocks appreciated, attracting more buying, and this led to further appreciation, in a process that as usual took on the appearance of an unstoppable virtuous circle.

Logical-seeming rationales play a part in most bull markets, and this one was no different: tech stocks will outperform all other stocks because of the companies' excellence. More tech names will be added to the equity indices, reflecting their growing importance in the economy. This will require index funds and the "closet indexers" who covertly emulate indices to buy more of them, and active investors will buy to keep up as well. More people will create 401(k) retirement plans, and 401(k) investors will increase the representation of stocks in their portfolios and the allocation to tech stocks among their stocks. For these reasons, tech stocks (a) must keep appreciating and (b) must outpace other stocks. Thus they'll attract still more buying. The fact that all of these phenomena actually occurred for a while lent credence to this theory.

Initial public offerings of technology stocks began to appreciate by tens and even hundreds of percent on the day of issue and took on the appearance of sure winners. Gaining access to IPOs became a popular mania.

From the perspective of psychology, what was happening with IPOs is particularly fascinating. It went something like this: The guy next to you in the office tells you about an IPO he's buying. You ask what the company does. He says he doesn't know, but his broker told him it's going to double on the day of issue. So you say that's ridiculous. A week later he tells you it didn't double . . . it tripled. And he still doesn't know what it does. After a few more of these, it gets hard to resist. You know it doesn't make sense, but you want protection against continuing to feel like an idiot. So, in a prime example of capitulation, you put in for a few hundred shares of the next IPO . . . and the bonfire grows still higher on the buying from new converts like you.

Venture capital funds that had invested in successful start-up companies attracted great attention and a great deal of capital. In the year Google went public, the fund that had seeded it appreciated 350 percent on the basis of that one success.

Tech stock investors were lauded by the media for their brilliance. The ones least restrained by experience and skepticism—and thus making the most money—were often in their thirties, even their twenties. Never was it pointed out that they might be beneficiaries of an irrational market rather than incredible astuteness.

Remember my earlier comment that all bubbles start with a modicum of truth? The seed of truth for the scenario just described lay in technology's very real potential. The fertilizer came from the attendant bullish rationales. And the supercharging came from the price appreciation that was taking place and looked unstoppable.

Of course, the entire furor over technology, e-commerce and telecom stocks stems from the companies' potential to change the world. I have absolutely no doubt that these movements are revolutionizing life as we know it, or that they will leave the world almost unrecognizable from what it was only a few years ago. The challenge lies in figuring out who the winners will be, and what a piece of them is really worth today. . . .

To say technology, Internet and telecommunications are too high and about to decline is comparable today to standing in front of a freight train. To say they have benefited from a boom of colossal proportions and should be examined skeptically is something I feel I owe you.

"BUBBLE.COM," JANUARY 3, 2000

Soon after the January 2000 memo was written, the tech stocks began to collapse of their own weight, even in the absence of any single event that would cause them to do so. All of a sudden it became clear that stock prices had gone too far and should correct. When an investment fad goes bad, *The Wall Street Journal* usually runs a table showing the resulting losses, with representative stocks down 90 percent or more. When the tech bubble burst, however, the table showed losses exceeding 99 percent. The broad stock indices experienced their first three-year decline since the Great

Depression, and tech stocks—and stocks in general—no longer looked like anything special.

When we look back over the intervening decade, we see that the vaunted technological developments did change the world, the winning companies are hugely valuable, and things like newspapers and CDs have been profoundly affected. But it's equally obvious that investors allowed their common sense to be overridden in the bubble. They ignored the fact that not all the companies could win, that there would be a lengthy shake-out period, that profitability wouldn't come easily from providing services gratis, and that shares in money-losing companies valued at high multiples of sales (since there were no earnings) carried great danger.

JOEL GREENBLATT: *Buffett's famous line about the economics of airlines comes to mind. Aviation is a huge and valuable innovation. That's not the same thing as saying it's a good business. Buffett said that a true capitalist would have shot down Wilbur in Kitty Hawk given the capital-destroying history of the aviation industry.*

Greed, excitement, illogicality, suspension of disbelief and ignoring value cost people a lot of money in the tech bubble. And, by the way, a lot of brilliant, disciplined value investors looked dumb in the months and years before the bubble burst—which of course it eventually did.

HOWARD MARKS: *The riskiest things: Positive feelings—sometimes called animal spirits—are major contributors to asset overpricing. Disciplined value investors look like pessimists, grumps, or old fogeys . . . until they turn out to be among of the few who protected against losses.*

To avoid losing money in bubbles, the key lies in refusing to join in when greed and human error cause positives to be wildly overrated and negatives to be ignored. Doing these things isn't easy, and thus few people are able to abstain. In just the same way, it's essential that investors avoid selling—and preferably should buy—when fear becomes excessive in a crash. (That reminds me to point out that bubbles are capable of arising on their own and need not be preceded by crashes, whereas crashes are invariably preceded by bubbles.)

As hard as it was for most people to resist buying in the tech bubble, it was even harder to resist selling—and still more difficult to buy—in the depths of the credit crisis. At worst, failing to buy in a bull market means you may look like a laggard and experience opportunity costs. But in the crash of 2008, the downside of failing to sell appeared to be unlimited loss. Armageddon actually seemed possible.

HOWARD MARKS: *Emotion and ego: Refusing to join in the errors of the herd—like so much else in investing—requires control over psyche and ego. It's the hardest thing, but the payoff can be enormous. Mastery over the human side of investing isn't sufficient for success, but combining it with analytical proficiency can lead to great results.*

What, in the end, are investors to do about these psychological urges that push them toward doing foolish things? Learn to see them for what they are; that's the first step toward gaining the courage to resist. And be realistic. Investors who believe they're immune to the forces described in this chapter do so at their own peril. If they influence others enough to move whole markets, why shouldn't they affect you, too? If a bull case is so powerful that it can make adults overlook elevated valuations and deny the impossibility of the perpetual-motion machine, why shouldn't it have the same influence on you? If a scare story of unlimited loss is strong enough to make others sell at giveaway prices, what would keep it from doing the same to you?

Believe me, it's hard to resist buying at the top (and harder still to sell) when everyone else is buying, the pundits are positive, the rationale is widely accepted, prices are soaring and the biggest risk takers are reporting huge returns. It's also hard to resist selling (and very tough to buy) when the opposite is true at the bottom and holding or buying appears to entail the risk of total loss.

HOWARD MARKS: *Fear of looking wrong: Remember, you're not going to be wrong in a vacuum. Assets go too far because of the actions of others. Just as you look wrong for a while, the members of the herd look (and feel) right. Comparing your lot with theirs is a very corrosive process—albeit natural—and will put a lot of pressure on you.*

Like so many other things described in this book, there's no simple solution: no formula that will tell you when the market has gone to an irrational extreme, no foolproof tool that will keep you on the right side of these decisions, no magic pill that will protect you against destructive emotions. As Charlie Munger says, "It's not supposed to be easy."

What weapons might you marshal on your side to increase your odds? Here are the ones that work for Oaktree:

- a strongly held sense of intrinsic value,

> **JOEL GREENBLATT:** *Without this, an investor has no home base. A strong sense of intrinsic value is the only way to withstand the psychological influences that affect behavior. Those who can't value companies or securities have no business investing and limited prospects (other than luck) for investing successfully. This sounds simple, but plenty of investors lack it.*

- insistence on acting as you should when price diverges from value,
- enough conversance with past cycles—gained at first from reading and talking to veteran investors, and later through experience—to know that market excesses are ultimately punished, not rewarded,
- a thorough understanding of the insidious effect of psychology on the investing process at market extremes,
- a promise to remember that when things seem "too good to be true," they usually are,
- willingness to look wrong while the market goes from misvalued to more misvalued (as it invariably will), and
- like-minded friends and colleagues from whom to gain support (and for you to support).

These things aren't sure to do the job, but they can give you a fighting chance.

11

The Most Important Thing Is . . . Contrarianism

> To buy when others are despondently selling and to sell when others are euphorically buying takes the greatest courage, but provides the greatest profit.
>
> SIR JOHN TEMPLETON

There's only one way to describe most investors: *trend followers*. Superior investors are the exact opposite. Superior investing, as I hope I've convinced you by now, requires second-level thinking—a way of thinking that's different from that of others, more complex and more insightful. By definition, most of the crowd can't share it. Thus, the judgments of the crowd can't hold the key to success. Rather, the trend, the consensus view, is something to game against, and the consensus portfolio is one to diverge from. As the pendulum swings or the market goes through its cycles, the key to ultimate success lies in doing the opposite.

This is the core of Warren Buffett's oft-quoted advice: "The less prudence with which others conduct their affairs, the greater the prudence with which we should conduct our own affairs." He is urging us to do the opposite of what others do: to be contrarians.

PAUL JOHNSON: *Contrarianism is an important skill for successful value investors. However, I have found that the most important ingredient to developing this skill is experience. Contrarianism is challenging to teach.*

Doing the same thing others do exposes you to fluctuations that in part are exaggerated by their actions and your own. It's certainly undesirable to be part of the herd when it stampedes off the cliff, but it takes rare skill, insight and discipline to avoid it.

"THE REALIST'S CREED," MAY 31, 2002

The logic of crowd error is clear and almost mathematical:

- Markets swing dramatically, from bullish to bearish and from over-priced to underpriced.
- Their movements are driven by the actions of "the crowd," "the herd" or "most people." Bull markets occur because more people want to buy than sell, or the buyers are more highly motivated than the sellers. The market rises as people switch from being sellers to being buyers, and as buyers become even more motivated and the sellers less so. (If buyers didn't predominate, the market wouldn't be rising.)

PAUL JOHNSON: *This is a key insight into one of the best ways to use contrarianism to one's favor.*

- Market extremes represent inflection points. These occur when bullishness or bearishness reaches a maximum. Figuratively speaking, a top occurs when the last person who will become a buyer does so. Since every buyer has joined the bullish herd by the time the top is reached, bullishness can go no further and the market is as high as it can go. Buying or holding is dangerous.
- Since there's no one left to turn bullish, the market stops going up. And if on the next day one person switches from buyer to seller, it will start to go down.
- So at the extremes, which are created by what "most people" believe, most people are wrong.
- Therefore, the key to investment success has to lie in doing the opposite: in diverging from the crowd. Those who recognize the errors that others make can profit enormously through contrarianism.

From time to time we see rabid buyers or terrified sellers; urgency to get in or to get out; overheated markets or ice-cold markets; and prices unsustainably high or ridiculously low. Certainly the markets, and investor attitudes and behavior, spend only a small portion of the time at "the happy medium."

What does this say about how we should act? Joining the herd and participating in the extremes of these cycles obviously can be dangerous to your financial health. The markets' extreme highs are created when avid buyers are in control, pushing prices to levels that may never be seen again. The lows are created when panicky sellers predominate, willing to part with assets at prices that often turn out to have been grossly inadequate.

"Buy low; sell high" is the time-honored dictum, but investors who are swept up in market cycles too often do just the opposite. The proper response lies in contrarian behavior: buy when they hate 'em, and sell when they love 'em. "Once-in-a-lifetime" market extremes seem to occur once every decade or so—not often enough for an investor to build a career around capitalizing on them. But attempting to do so should be an important component of any investor's approach.

JOEL GREENBLATT: *I love this thought. Extreme circumstances (or, more accurately, opportunities) occur more often than seems reasonable. You never catch the bottom or the top of these situations, and that's where the pain and degree of difficulty come in!*

Just don't think it'll be easy. You need the ability to detect instances in which prices have diverged significantly from intrinsic value. You have to have a strong-enough stomach to defy conventional wisdom (one of the greatest oxymorons) and resist the myth that the market's always efficient and thus right. You need experience on which to base this resolute behavior. And you must have the support of understanding, patient constituencies. Without enough time to ride out the extremes while waiting for reason to prevail, you'll become that most typical of market victims: the six-foot-tall man who drowned crossing the stream that was five feet deep on average.

JOEL GREENBLATT: *One of Buffett's and Marks's greatest concepts. In the long run, the market gets it right. But you have to survive over the short run, to get to the long run.*

But if you're alert to the pendulum-like swing of the markets, it's possible to recognize the opportunities that occasionally are there for the plucking.

"THE HAPPY MEDIUM," JULY 21, 2004

~

Accepting the broad concept of contrarianism is one thing; putting it into practice is another. On one hand, we never know how far the pendulum will swing, when it will reverse, and how far it will then go in the opposite direction.

On the other hand, we can be sure that, once it reaches an extreme position, the market eventually will swing back toward the midpoint (or beyond). Investors who believed that the pendulum would move in one direction forever—or, having reached an extreme, would stay there—are inevitably disappointed.

On the third hand, however, because of the variability of the many factors that influence markets, no tool—not even contrarianism—can be relied on completely.

- Contrarianism isn't an approach that will make you money all of the time. Much of the time there aren't great market excesses to bet against.

> **JOEL GREENBLATT:** *I've put it this way: just because no one else will jump in front of a Mack truck barreling down the highway, doesn't mean that you should!*

- Even when an excess does develop, it's important to remember that "overpriced" is incredibly different from "going down tomorrow."
- Markets can be over- or underpriced and stay that way—or become more so—for years.
- It can be extremely painful when the trend is going against you.

> **SETH KLARMAN:** *This is where it is particularly important to remember the teachings of Graham and Dodd. If you look to the markets for a report card, owning a stock that declines every day will make you feel like a failure. But if you remember that you own a fractional interest in a business and that every day you are able to*

buy in at a greater discount to underlying value, you might just be able to maintain a cheerful disposition. This is exactly how Warren Buffett describes bargain hunting amid the ravages of the 1973 to 1974 bear market.

- It can appear at times that "everyone" has reached the conclusion that the herd is wrong. What I mean is that contrarianism itself can appear to have become too popular, and thus contrarianism can be mistaken for herd behavior.
- Finally, it's not enough to bet against the crowd. Given the difficulties associated with contrarianism just mentioned, the potentially profitable recognition of divergences from consensus thinking must be based on reason and analysis. You must do things not just because they're the opposite of what the crowd is doing, but because you know why the crowd is wrong. Only then will you be able to hold firmly to your views and perhaps buy more as your positions take on the appearance of mistakes and as losses accrue rather than gains.

David Swensen heads the Yale University endowment. Yale's investment performance has been outstanding, and Swensen has had a greater impact on endowment investing than anyone else over the last two decades. His thinking, which was highly unusual when Yale began to implement it in the 1980s, came to represent endowment canon. He has a beautiful way of describing the difficulties associated with contrarianism.

Investment success requires sticking with positions made uncomfortable by their variance with popular opinion. Casual commitments invite casual reversal, exposing portfolio managers to the damaging whipsaw of buying high and selling low. Only with the confidence created by a strong decision-making process can investors sell speculative excess and buy despair-driven value.

. . . Active management strategies demand uninstitutional behavior from institutions, creating a paradox that few can unravel. Establishing and maintaining an unconventional investment profile requires acceptance of uncomfortably idiosyncratic portfolios, which frequently appear downright imprudent in the eyes of conventional wisdom.

PIONEERING PORTFOLIO MANAGEMENT, 2000

The ultimately most profitable investment actions are by definition contrarian: you're buying when everyone else is selling (and the price is thus low) or you're selling when everyone else is buying (and the price is high).

PAUL JOHNSON: *The reward for successfully following Marks's advice is well articulated here.*

These actions are lonely and, as Swensen says, uncomfortable. How can we know it's the opposite—the consensus action—that's the comfortable one? Because most people are doing it.

HOWARD MARKS: *Fear of looking wrong: The very words used here—uninstitutional, idiosyncratic, imprudent, lonely, and uncomfortable—provide an idea of how challenging it is to maintain non-consensus positions. But doing so is an absolute must if superior performance is to be achieved.*

~

The thing I find most interesting about investing is how paradoxical it is: how often the things that seem most obvious—on which everyone agrees—turn out not to be true.

I'm not saying accepted investment wisdom is sometimes valid and sometimes not. The reality is simpler and much more systematic: Most people don't understand the process through which something comes to have outstanding moneymaking potential.

What's clear to the broad consensus of investors is almost always wrong. . . . The very coalescing of popular opinion behind an investment tends to eliminate its profit potential. . . . Take, for example, the investment that "everyone" believes to be a great idea. In my view by definition it simply cannot be so.

- If everyone likes it, it's probably because it has been doing well. Most people seem to think outstanding performance to date presages outstanding future performance. Actually, it's more likely that outstanding performance to date has borrowed from the future and thus presages subpar performance from here on out.

JOEL GREENBLATT: *This is extremely simple and extremely insightful.*

- If everyone likes it, it's likely the price has risen to reflect a level of adulation from which relatively little further appreciation is likely. (Sure, it's possible for something to move from "overvalued" to "more overvalued," but I wouldn't want to count on it happening.)
- If everyone likes it, it's likely the area has been mined too thoroughly—and has seen too much capital flow in—for many bargains to remain.
- If everyone likes it, there's significant risk that prices will fall if the crowd changes its collective mind and moves for the exit.

Superior investors know—and buy—when the price of something is lower than it should be. And the price of an investment can be lower than it should be only when most people don't see its merit. Yogi Berra is famous for having said, "Nobody goes to that restaurant anymore; it's too crowded." It's just as nonsensical to say, "Everyone realizes that investment's a bargain." If everyone realizes it, they'll buy, in which case the price will no longer be low. . . . Large amounts of money aren't made by buying what everybody likes. They're made by buying what everybody underestimates. . . .

In short, there are two primary elements in superior investing:

- seeing some quality that others don't see or appreciate (and that isn't reflected in the price), and
- having it turn out to be true (or at least accepted by the market).

It should be clear from the first element that the process has to begin with investors who are unusually perceptive, unconventional, iconoclastic or early. That's why successful investors are said to spend a lot of their time being lonely.

"EVERYONE KNOWS," APRIL 26, 2007

The global credit crisis of 2007–2008 represents the greatest crash I have ever seen. The lessons to be learned from this experience are many, which is one reason I discuss aspects of it in more than one chapter. For me, one such lesson consisted of reaching a new understanding of the skepticism required for contrarian thinking. I'm not usually given to epiphanies, but I had one on the subject of skepticism.

Every time a bubble bursts, a bull market collapses or a silver bullet fails to work, we hear people bemoan their error. The skeptic, highly aware of that, tries to identify delusions ahead of time and avoid falling into line with the crowd in accepting them. So, usually, investment skepticism is associated with rejecting investment fads, bull market manias and Ponzi schemes.

My epiphany came in mid-October 2008, near the low point of the global credit meltdown. By then we were seeing and hearing things that we never imagined possible:

- The demise or bailout of Lehman Brothers, Bear Stearns, Freddie Mac, Fannie Mae and AIG
- Concern about the viability of Goldman Sachs and Morgan Stanley, and huge declines in their stocks
- Rising prices for credit-default-swap protection on U.S. Treasury securities
- Rates on short-term T-bills close to zero because of an extreme flight to safety
- Awareness for the first time, I think, that the U.S. government's financial resources are finite and that there are limits on its ability to run the printing press and solve problems

It was readily apparent immediately after the bankruptcy of Lehman Brothers that . . . a spiral was under way, and no one could see how or when it might end. That was really the problem: no scenario was too negative to be credible, and any scenario incorporating an element of optimism was dismissed as Pollyannaish.

There was an element of truth in this, of course: nothing was impossible. But in dealing with the future, we must think about two things: (a) what might happen and (b) the probability that it will happen.

During the crisis, lots of bad things seemed possible, but that didn't mean they were going to happen. In times of crisis, people fail to make that distinction. . . .

For forty years I've seen the manic-depressive pendulum of investor psychology swing crazily: between fear and greed—we all know the refrain—but also between optimism and pessimism, and between credulity and skepticism. In general, following the beliefs of the herd—and swinging with the pendulum—will give you average performance in the long run and can get you killed at the extremes. . . .

///

JOEL GREENBLATT: *Investor sentiment was extreme in October 2008. Valuations were incredibly cheap, and stocks offered wonderful returns looking forward. In fact, over the next two years returns were spectacular. Unfortunately, stocks first fell another 20 percent from the already low October 2008 levels before they eventually turned around (in March 2009).*

\\\

If you believe the story everyone else believes, you'll do what they do. Usually you'll buy at high prices and sell at lows. You'll fall for tales of the "silver bullet" capable of delivering high returns without risk. You'll buy what's been doing well and sell what's been doing poorly. And you'll suffer losses in crashes and miss out when things recover from bottoms. In other words, you'll be a conformist, not a maverick; a follower, not a contrarian.

Skepticism is what it takes to look behind a balance sheet, the latest miracle of financial engineering or the can't-miss story. . . . Only a skeptic can separate the things that sound good and are from the things that sound good and aren't. The best investors I know exemplify this trait. It's an absolute necessity.

Lots of bad things happened to kick off the credit crisis that had been considered unlikely (if not impossible), and they happened at the same time, to investors who'd taken on significant leverage. So the easy explanation is that the people who were hurt in the credit crisis hadn't been skeptical—or pessimistic—enough.

But that triggered an epiphany: *skepticism and pessimism aren't synonymous.* Skepticism calls for pessimism when optimism is excessive. But it also calls for optimism when pessimism is excessive.

As the credit crisis reached a peak last week, . . . I found very few who were optimistic; most were pessimistic to some degree.

No one applied skepticism, or said "that horror story's unlikely to be true." The one thing they weren't doing last week was making aggressive bids for securities. So prices fell and fell—the old expression is "gapped down"—several points at a time.

The key—as usual—was to become skeptical of what "everyone" was saying and doing. The negative story may have looked compelling, but it's the positive story—which few believed—that held, and still holds, the greater potential for profit.

"THE LIMITS TO NEGATIVISM," OCTOBER 15, 2008

∿

The error is clear. The herd applies optimism at the top and pessimism at the bottom. Thus, to benefit, we must be skeptical of the optimism that thrives at the top, and skeptical of the pessimism that prevails at the bottom.

"TOUCHSTONES," NOVEMBER 10, 2009

Skepticism is usually thought to consist of saying, "no, that's too good to be true" at the right times. But I realized in 2008—and in retrospect it seems so obvious—that sometimes skepticism requires us to say, "no, that's too *bad* to be true."

Most purchases of depressed, distressed debt made in the fourth quarter of 2008 yielded returns of 50 to 100 percent or more over the next eighteen months. Buying was extremely difficult under those trying circumstances, but it was made easier when we realized that almost no one was saying, "no, things can't be that bad." At that moment, being optimistic and buying was the ultimate act of contrarianism.

∿

Certain common threads run through the best investments I've witnessed. They're usually contrarian, challenging and uncomfortable—although the experienced contrarian takes comfort from his or her position outside the herd.

HOWARD MARKS: *Fear of looking wrong: Not only should the lonely and uncomfortable position be tolerated, it should be celebrated. Usually—and certainly at the extremes of the pendulum's swing—being part of the herd should be a reason for worry.*

Whenever the debt market collapses, for example, most people say, "We're not going to try to catch a falling knife; it's too dangerous." They usually add, "We're going to wait until the dust settles and the uncertainty is resolved." What they mean, of course, is that they're frightened and unsure of what to do.

The one thing I'm sure of is that by the time the knife has stopped falling, the dust has settled and the uncertainty has been resolved, there'll be no great bargains left. When buying something has become comfortable again, its price will no longer be so low that it's a great bargain.

SETH KLARMAN: *And the high volumes that accompany a sharp selloff will also likely be over. Not only will prices be on the rebound, but buying a sizeable position will be much harder.*

Thus, a hugely profitable investment that doesn't begin with discomfort is usually an oxymoron.

It's our job as contrarians to catch falling knives, hopefully with care and skill. That's why the concept of intrinsic value is so important. If we hold a view of value that enables us to buy when everyone else is selling—and if our view turns out to be right—that's the route to the greatest rewards earned with the least risk.

12

The Most Important Thing Is . . . Finding Bargains

The best opportunities are usually found among things most others won't do.

The process of intelligently building a portfolio consists of buying the best investments, making room for them by selling lesser ones, and staying clear of the worst. The raw materials for the process consist of (a) a list of potential investments, (b) estimates of their intrinsic value, (c) a sense for how their prices compare with their intrinsic value, and (d) an understanding of the risks involved in each, and of the effect their inclusion would have on the portfolio being assembled.

CHRISTOPHER DAVIS: *This is a great summary.*

The first step is usually to make sure that the things being considered satisfy some absolute standards. Even sophisticated investors may not say, "I'll buy anything if it's cheap enough." More often they create a list of investment candidates meeting their minimum criteria, and from those they choose the best bargains. That's what this chapter is all about.

For example, an investor might start by narrowing the list of possibilities to those whose riskiness falls within acceptable limits, since there can be risks with which certain investors aren't comfortable. Examples might include the risk of obsolescence in a fast-moving segment of the technology world, and the risk that a hot consumer product will lose its popularity; these might be subjects that some investors consider beyond their expertise. Or investors might find some companies unacceptable in the absolute because their industries are too unpredictable or their financial statements aren't sufficiently transparent.

It's not unreasonable to want to emphasize assets that fall within a certain portion of the risk spectrum. Securities that the market deems ultrasafe may offer uninteresting returns, while securities at the other extreme may exceed investors' risk tolerance. In other words, there can reasonably be some places investors won't go, regardless of price.

CHRISTOPHER DAVIS: *These are good caveats to Marks's earlier discussions of price and risk.*

Not only can there be risks investors don't want to take, but also there can be risks their clients don't want them to take. Especially in the institutional world, managers are rarely told "Here's my money; do what you want with it." The money manager's job isn't just to make investments with profit potential, but also to give clients what they want, since most institutional investors are hired to carry out specific assignments in terms of asset class and investment style.

CHRISTOPHER DAVIS: *This is a realistic description of a money manager's job, but I still think it's important for managers not to become overly cautious as this attitude can easily turn into a paralyzing fear of headline risk or controversy.*

If the client came for one kind of investment, there's little to be gained in going into others, regardless of their attractiveness. For example, if a manager solicits accounts on the basis of expertise in high-quality, large-capitalization value stocks, there's risk to the business in investing in a bunch of high-tech start-ups.

Thus, the starting point for portfolio construction is unlikely to be an unbounded universe. Some things are realistic candidates for inclusion, and others aren't.

~

Having defined the "feasible set," the next step is to select investments from it. That's done by identifying those that offer the best ratio of potential return to risk, or the most value for the money. That's what Sid Cottle, editor of the later editions of Graham and Dodd's *Security Analysis*, was talking about when he told me that in his view, "investment is the discipline of relative selection." That expression has stayed with me for thirty-five years.

Sid's simple phrase embodies two important messages. First, the process of investing has to be rigorous and disciplined. Second, it is by necessity comparative. Whether prices are depressed or elevated, and whether prospective returns are therefore high or low, we have to find the best investments out there. Since we can't change the market, if we want to participate, our only option is to select the best from the possibilities that exist. These are relative decisions.

> **JOEL GREENBLATT:** *With some investment experience, it may be possible to compare current investment opportunities that appear to be relative bargains to valuation-based bargains that were available in the past. In this way, available opportunities that appear to be relative bargains based on the current opportunity set can be compared to a potential future set of bargain opportunities as well.*

~

What is it that makes something the superior investment we look for? As I mentioned in chapter 4, it's largely a matter of price. Our goal isn't to find good assets, but good buys. Thus, it's not what you buy; it's what you pay for it.

> **CHRISTOPHER DAVIS:** *This is subject to the risk and selection criteria mentioned above.*

A high-quality asset can constitute a good or bad buy, and a low-quality asset can constitute a good or bad buy. The tendency to mistake objective merit for investment opportunity, and the failure to distinguish between good assets and good buys, get most investors into trouble.

///

CHRISTOPHER DAVIS: *Agreed!*

\\

Because the search is for good buys, my main goal in this chapter is to explain what makes a buy a good one. In general, that means price is low relative to value, and potential return is high relative to risk. How do bargains get that way?

In chapter 10, I used the tech-stock mania as an example of the reliable process through which a good fundamental idea can be turned into an overpriced bubble. It usually starts with an objectively attractive asset. As people raise their opinion of it, they increasingly want to own it. That makes capital flow to it, and the price rises. People take the rising price as a sign of the investment's merit, so they buy still more. Others hear about it for the first time and join in, and the upward trend takes on the appearance of an unstoppable virtuous cycle. It's mostly a popularity contest in which the asset in question is the winner.

If they go on long enough and gain enough force, investment styles turn into bubbles. And bubbles give thoughtful investors lots of things to sell and sell short.

The process through which bargains are created is largely the opposite. Thus to be able to find them, it's essential that we understand what causes an asset to be out of favor. This isn't necessarily the result of an analytical process. In fact, much of the process is anti-analytical, meaning it's important to think about the psychological forces behind it and the changes in popularity that drive it.

So what is it that makes price low relative to value, and return high relative to risk? In other words, what makes something sell cheaper than it should?

- Unlike assets that become the subject of manias, potential bargains usually display some objective defect. An asset class may have weaknesses, a company may be a laggard in its industry, a balance sheet may be over-levered, or a security may afford its holders inadequate structural protection.
- Since the efficient-market process of setting fair prices requires the involvement of people who are analytical and objective, bargains usually

are based on irrationality or incomplete understanding. Thus, bargains are often created when investors either fail to consider an asset fairly, or fail to look beneath the surface to understand it thoroughly, or fail to overcome some non-value-based tradition, bias or stricture.

- Unlike market darlings, the orphan asset is ignored or scorned. To the extent it's mentioned at all by the media and at cocktail parties, it's in unflattering terms.

///

SETH KLARMAN: *Generally, the greater the stigma or revulsion, the better the bargain.*

\\\

- Usually its price has been falling, making the first-level thinker ask, "Who would want to own that?" (It bears repeating that most investors extrapolate past performance, expecting the continuation of trends rather than the far-more-dependable *regression to the mean*. First-level thinkers tend to view past price weakness as worrisome, not as a sign that the asset has gotten cheaper.)
- As a result, a bargain asset tends to be one that's highly unpopular. Capital stays away from it or flees, and no one can think of a reason to own it.

Here's an example of how bargains can be created when an entire asset class goes out of style.

The story of bonds in the last sixty years is the mirror opposite of the rise in popularity enjoyed by stocks. First bonds wilted as stocks monopolized the spotlight in the fifties and sixties, and at the end of 1969, First National City Bank's weekly summary of bond data died with the heading "The Last Issue" boxed in black. Bonds were decimated in the high-interest-rate environment of the seventies, and even though interest rates declined steadily during the eighties and nineties, bonds didn't have a prayer of standing up to equities' dramatic gains.

By the latter half of the nineties, any investment in bonds rather than stocks felt like an anchor restraining performance. I chaired the investment committee of a charity and watched as a sister organization in another city—which had suffered for years

with an 80:20 bond/stock mix—shifted its allocation to 0:100.
I imagined a typical institutional investor saying the following:

> We have a small allocation to fixed income. I can't tell you
> why. It's a historical accident. My predecessor created it,
> but his reasons are lost in the past. Now our bond hold-
> ings are under review for reduction.

Even though interest in buying more stocks remained low in the
current decade, little money flowed to high grade bonds. The continued decline in bonds' popularity was caused, among other
things, by the decision on the part of the Greenspan Fed to keep
interest rates low to stimulate the economy and combat exogenous
shocks (like the Y2K scare). With Treasurys and high grade bonds
yielding 3–4 percent, they didn't do much for institutional investors trying for 8 percent.

"HEMLINES," SEPTEMBER 10, 2010

After the process described above had gone on long enough, and holdings of them had been reduced enough, bonds were positioned to become
superior performers. All it took was a change in the environment that would
increase the desirability of safety relative to upside potential. And as usually
happens after an asset has appreciated for a while, investors suddenly recognized the attractions of bonds and realized they didn't own enough. This
is a pattern that regularly produces profits for those who figure it out early.

∿

Fairly priced assets are never our objective, since it's reasonable to conclude they'll deliver just fair returns for the risk involved. And, of course,
overpriced assets don't do us any good.

Our goal is to find underpriced assets. Where should we look for them?
A good place to start is among things that are:

- little known and not fully understood;
- fundamentally questionable on the surface;
- controversial, unseemly or scary;
- deemed inappropriate for "respectable" portfolios;

- unappreciated, unpopular and unloved;
- trailing a record of poor returns; and
- recently the subject of disinvestment, not accumulation.

PAUL JOHNSON: *This is an excellent "shopping list."*

To boil it all down to just one sentence, I'd say the necessary condition for the existence of bargains is that perception has to be considerably worse than reality. That means the best opportunities are usually found among things most others won't do. After all, if everyone feels good about something and is glad to join in, it won't be bargain-priced.

When I shifted from equity research to portfolio management at Citibank in 1978, I was fortunate to be asked to work in asset classes that met some or all of these criteria. My first assignment was in convertible securities. These were even more of a small and underappreciated market backwater than they are now. Since they gave investors the advantages of both bonds and stocks, they were issued only as a last resort by weak companies lacking alternatives, such as conglomerates, railroads and airlines. Mainstream investors felt they introduced unnecessary complexity: if you want the characteristics of bonds and stocks, they might say, why not just buy some bonds and some stocks? And if you like the company, why not buy the stock and garner its entire return, rather than investing in a defensive hybrid vehicle? Well, whenever "everyone" feels there's no merit in something, it's reasonable to suspect it's unloved, unpursued and thus possibly underpriced. That's why a 1984 *BusinessWeek* article about me carried the line "Real men don't buy converts, so chickens like me can buy cheap."

Later in 1978, I was asked to start a fund for high yield bonds. These low-rated securities, burdened with the unpleasant sobriquet *junk bonds*, fell short of most investing institutions' minimum requirement of "investment grade or better" or "single-A or better." Junk bonds might default, so how could they possibly be appropriate holdings for pension funds or endowments? And if a fund bought a bond from a speculative-grade company and it went under, how could the trustees escape embarrassment and blame for having done something that they knew in advance was risky?

CHRISTOPHER DAVIS: *The same is also true of headline risk.*

A great clue to these securities' potential could be found in one rating agency's description of B-rated bonds as "generally lacking the character-istics of a desirable investment." By now you should be quick to ask how anyone could issue a blanket dismissal of a potential class of investments without any reference to price.

SETH KLARMAN: *More broadly, this is the problem with all agency ratings. The supposed safety attracts investors who fail to do their own homework, making them the ultimate buyers of conventional wisdom. Ironically, ratings downgrades typically occur long after the markets have figured out that a problem exists, leaving inves-tors who trusted the ratings with large losses.*

The subsequent history of these bonds shows that (a) if nobody owns something, demand for it (and thus the price) can only go up and (b) by go-ing from taboo to even just tolerated, it can perform quite well.

Finally, in 1987, my partners Bruce Karsh and Sheldon Stone came to me with the bright idea of forming a fund to invest in distressed debt. What could possibly be more unseemly and less respectable than investing in the bonds of companies that are bankrupt or deemed overwhelmingly likely to become so? Who would invest in companies that already had demonstrated their lack of financial viability and the weakness of their management? How could anyone invest responsibly in companies in free fall? Of course, given the way investors behave, whatever asset is consid-ered the worst at a given point in time has a good likelihood of being the cheapest.

PAUL JOHNSON: *This is a nice litmus test for finding bargains.*

Investment bargains needn't have anything to do with high quality. In fact, things tend to be cheaper if low quality has scared people away.

Each of these asset classes satisfied most or all of the criteria listed earlier in this chapter. They were little known, not understood and not respected. No one had a good word to say about any of them. Each exem-plified the uncomfortably idiosyncratic and imprudent-appearing in-vestments that David Swensen talked about in chapter 11 . . . and thus each turned into a great place to be for the next twenty or thirty years.

I hope these large-scale examples give you a good idea for where bargains may be found.

JOEL GREENBLATT: *Marks's description outlines the opportunities for both value and special-situation investing in general.*

~

Since bargains provide value at unreasonably low prices—and thus unusual ratios of return to risk—they represent the Holy Grail for investors. Such deals shouldn't exist in an efficient market for the reasons specified in chapter 2. However, everything in my experience tells me that while bargains aren't the rule, the forces that are supposed to eliminate them often fail to do so.

We're active investors because we believe we can beat the market by identifying superior opportunities. On the other hand, many of the "special deals" we're offered are too good to be true, and avoiding them is essential for investment success. Thus, as with so many things, the optimism that drives one to be an active investor and the skepticism that emerges from the presumption of market efficiency must be balanced.

It's obvious that investors can be forced into mistakes by psychological weakness, analytical error or refusal to tread on uncertain ground. Those mistakes create bargains for second-level thinkers capable of seeing the errors of others.

13

The Most Important Thing Is . . . Patient Opportunism

The market's not a very accommodating machine; it won't provide high returns just because you need them.

PETER BERNSTEIN

The boom-bust cycle associated with the global financial crisis gave us the chance to sell at highly elevated levels in the period 2005 through early 2007 and then to buy at panic prices in late 2007 and 2008. This was in many ways the chance of a lifetime. Cycle-fighting contrarians had a golden opportunity to distinguish themselves. But one of the things I want to do in this chapter is to point out that there aren't always great things to do, and sometimes we maximize our contribution by being discerning and relatively inactive. Patient opportunism—waiting for bargains—is often your best strategy.

PAUL JOHNSON: *Marks offers great wisdom in this chapter. The challenge is that many investors confuse action for adding value when, in fact, all of the studies suggest that most investors over-trade their portfolio. Compounding the challenge, it is not clear that human beings are naturally wired to be patient.*

So here's a tip: You'll do better if you wait for investments to come to you rather than go chasing after them. You tend to get better buys if you select from the list of things sellers are motivated to sell rather than start with a fixed notion as to what you want to own. An opportunist buys things because they're offered at bargain prices. There's nothing special about buying when prices aren't low.

At Oaktree, one of our mottos is "we don't look for our investments; they find us." We try to sit on our hands. We don't go out with a "buy list"; rather, we wait for the phone to ring. If we call the owner and say, "You own X and we want to buy it," the price will go up. But if the owner calls us and says, "We're stuck with X and we're looking for an exit," the price will go down. Thus, rather than initiating transactions, we prefer to react opportunistically.

At any particular point in time, the investment environment is a given, and we have no alternative other than to accept it and invest within it. There isn't always a pendulum or cycle extreme to bet against. Sometimes greed and fear, optimism and pessimism, and credulousness and skepticism are balanced, and thus clear mistakes aren't being made. Rather than obviously overpriced or underpriced, most things may seem roughly fairly priced. In that case, there may not be great bargains to buy or compelling sales to make.

JOEL GREENBLATT: *This is one of the hardest things to master for professional investors: coming in each day for work and doing nothing.*

It's essential for investment success that we recognize the condition of the market and decide on our actions accordingly. The other possibilities are (a) acting without recognizing the market's status, (b) acting with indifference to its status and (c) believing we can somehow change its status. These are most unwise. It makes perfect sense that we must invest appropriately for the circumstances with which we're presented. In fact, nothing else makes sense at all.

I come to this from a philosophic foundation:

In the mid-sixties, Wharton students had to have a nonbusiness minor, and I satisfied the requirement by taking five courses in Japanese studies. These surprised me by becoming the highlight of my college career, and later they contributed to my investment philosophy in a major way.

Among the values prized in early Japanese culture was *mujo*. *Mujo* was defined classically for me as recognition of "the turning of the wheel of the law," implying acceptance of the inevitability of change, of rise and fall. . . . In other words, *mujo* means cycles will rise and fall, things will come and go, and our environment will change in ways beyond our control. Thus we must recognize, accept, cope and respond. Isn't that the essence of investing?

. . . What's past is past and can't be undone. It has led to the circumstances we now face. All we can do is recognize our circumstances for what they are and make the best decisions we can, given the givens.

"IT IS WHAT IT IS," MARCH 27, 2006

Warren Buffett's philosophy is a little less spiritually based than mine. Instead of *mujo*, his reference is to baseball.

In Berkshire Hathaway's 1997 Annual Report, Buffett talked about Ted Williams—the "Splendid Splinter"—one of the greatest hitters in history. A factor that contributed to his success was his intensive study of his own game. By breaking down the strike zone into 77 baseball-sized "cells" and charting his results at the plate, he learned that his batting average was much better when he went after only pitches in his "sweet spot." Of course, even with that knowledge, he couldn't wait all day for the perfect pitch; if he let three strikes go by without swinging, he'd be called out.

Way back in the November 1, 1974, issue of *Forbes*, Buffett pointed out that investors have an advantage in that regard, if they'll just seize it. Because they can't strike out looking, investors needn't feel pressured to act. They can pass up lots of opportunities until they see one that's terrific.

Investing is the greatest business in the world because you never have to swing. You stand at the plate; the pitcher throws you General Motors at 47! U.S. Steel at 39! And nobody calls a strike on you. There's no penalty except opportunity. All day you wait for the pitch you like; then, when the fielders are asleep, you step up and hit it.

"WHAT'S YOUR GAME PLAN?" SEPTEMBER 5, 2003

JOEL GREENBLATT: *I think of this analogy often (especially when I'm feeling a little lazy).*

One of the great things about investing is that the only real penalty is for making losing investments. There's no penalty for omitting losing investments, of course, just rewards. And even for missing a few winners, the penalty is bearable.

SETH KLARMAN: *Still, calibration is important. Set the bar too high and you might remain out of the market for a very long time. Set it too low and you will be fully invested almost immediately; it will be as though you had no standards at all. Experience and versatile thinking are the keys to such calibration.*

Where does the penalty for missing winners come in? Well, investors are generally competitive and in it for the money. Thus, no one's totally comfortable with missing a profitable opportunity.

For professional investors paid to manage others' money, the stakes are higher. If they miss too many opportunities, and if their returns are too low in good times, money managers can come under pressure from clients and eventually lose accounts. A lot depends on how clients have been conditioned.

CHRISTOPHER DAVIS: *The key is managing clients effectively—which almost always means lowering client expectations.*

Oaktree has always been explicit about our belief that missing a profitable opportunity is of less significance than investing in a loser. Thus, our clients are prepared for results that put risk control ahead of full participation in gains.

///

JOEL GREENBLATT: *We may look through fifty or seventy invest-ments to find a handful of good ones. If we buy six that work out and miss fifteen that we should have bought, we never view this as a loss.*

\\\

~

Standing at the plate with the bat on your shoulders is Buffett's version of patient opportunism. The bat should come off our shoulders when there are opportunities for profit with controlled risk, but only then. One way to be selective in this regard is by making every effort to ascertain whether we're in a low-return environment or a high-return environment.

A few years ago I came up with an allegory applicable to low-return environments. It was called "The Cat, the Tree, the Carrot and the Stick." The cat is an investor, whose job it is to cope with the investment environment, of which the tree is part. The carrot—the incentive to accept increased risk—comes from the higher returns seemingly available from riskier investments. And the stick—the motivation to forsake safety—comes from the modest level of the prospective returns being offered on safer investments.

The carrot lures the cat to higher branches—riskier strategies—in pursuit of its dinner (its targeted return), and the stick prods the cat up the tree, because it can't get dinner while staying close to the ground.

Together, the stick and the carrot can cause the cat to climb until it ultimately arrives high up in the tree, in a treacherous position. The critical observation is that the cat pursues high returns, even in a low-return environment, and bears the consequences—increased risk—although often unknowingly.

Bond investors call this process "reaching for yield" or "reaching for return." It has classically consisted of investing in riskier credits as the yields on safer ones decline, in order to access the returns to which investors were accustomed before the market rose. That same pattern of taking new and bigger risks in order to perpetuate return often repeats in a cyclical pattern. The motto of those who reach for return seems to be: "If you can't get the return you need from safe investments, pursue it via risky investments."

We saw this behavior playing out in the middle of the past decade:

> [In the days before the credit crisis], investors succumbed to the si-ren song of leverage. They borrowed cheap short-term funds—the shorter the cheaper (you can get money cheap if you're willing to promise repayment monthly). And they used that money to buy assets that offered higher returns because they entailed illiquidity and/or fundamental risk. And institutional investors all over the world took Wall Street up on the newest promises of two "silver bullets" that would provide high returns with low risk: securitiza-tion and structure.
>
> On the surface, these investments made sense. They prom-ised satisfactory absolute returns, as the returns on the levered purchases would more than pay the cost of capital. The results would be great . . . as long as nothing untoward happened.
>
> But, as usual, the pursuit of profit led to mistakes. The expected returns looked good, but the range of possible outcomes included some very nasty ones. The success of many techniques and struc-tures depended on the future looking like the past. And many of the "modern miracles" that were relied on were untested.
>
> "NO DIFFERENT THIS TIME," DECEMBER 17, 2007

It's remarkable how many leading competitors from our early years as investors are no longer leading competitors (or competitors at all). While a number faltered because of flaws in their organization or business model, others disappeared because they insisted on pursuing high returns in low-return environments.

You simply cannot create investment opportunities when they're not there. The dumbest thing you can do is to insist on perpetuating high returns—and give back your profits in the process. If it's not there, hoping won't make it so.

When prices are high, it's inescapable that prospective returns are low (and risks are high).

CHRISTOPHER DAVIS: *And again: a high price both increases risk and lowers return.*

That single sentence provides a great deal of guidance as to appropriate portfolio actions. How are we to factor such an observation into our practices?

In 2004 I wrote a memo titled "Risk and Return Today." In it, as described in chapter 6, I expressed my view that (a) the capital market line then was "low and flat," meaning prospective returns in almost all markets were among the lowest we'd ever seen and risk premiums were the narrowest, and (b) if prospective returns should rise, it'd likely happen through price declines.

But the hard question is, what can we do about it? A few weeks later, I suggested a few possibilities:

How might one cope in a market that seems to be offering low returns?

- *Invest as if it's not true.* The trouble with this is that "wishing won't make it so." Simply put, it doesn't make sense to expect traditional returns when elevated asset prices suggest they're not available. I was pleased to get a letter from Peter Bernstein in response to my memo, in which he said something wonderful: "The market's not a very accommodating machine; it won't provide high returns just because you need them."

JOEL GREENBLATT: *A great statement.*

- *Invest anyway*—trying for acceptable relative returns under the circumstances, even if they're not attractive in the absolute.
- *Invest anyway*—ignoring short-run risk and focusing on the long run. This isn't irrational, especially if you accept the notion that market timing and tactical asset allocation are difficult. But before taking this path, I'd suggest that you get a commitment from your investment committee or other constituents that they'll ignore short-term losses.
- *Hold cash*—but that's tough for people who need to meet an actuarial assumption or spending rate; who want their money to be "fully employed" at all times; or who'll be uncomfortable (or lose their jobs) if they have to watch for long as others make money they don't.

//

SETH KLARMAN: *In recent years, holding cash is so completely out of favor that it has become the ultimate contrarian investment.*

\\\

- *Concentrate your investments in "special niches and special people,"* as I've been droning on about for the last couple of years. But that gets harder as the size of your portfolio grows. And identifying managers with truly superior talent, discipline and staying power certainly isn't easy.

The truth is, there's no easy answer for investors faced with skimpy prospective returns and risk premiums. But there is one course of action—one classic mistake—that I most strongly feel is wrong: reaching for return.

Given today's paucity of prospective return at the low-risk end of the spectrum and the solutions being ballyhooed at the high-risk end, many investors are moving capital to riskier (or at least less traditional) investments. But (a) they're making those riskier investments just when the prospective returns on those investments are the lowest they've ever been; (b) they're accepting return increments for stepping up in risk that are as slim as they've ever been; and (c) they're signing up today for things they turned down (or did less of) in the past, when the prospective returns were much higher. This may be exactly the wrong time to add to risk in pursuit of more return. You want to take risk when others are fleeing from it, not when they're competing with you to do so.

"THERE THEY GO AGAIN," MAY 6, 2005

//

SETH KLARMAN: *This highlights one of the pitfalls of investing with a return requirement, as corporate pension funds are forced to do. Trying to earn aggressive returns not only doesn't ensure that you will achieve them but also increases the likelihood that by making increasingly risky investments you will incur losses and fall far short, exacerbating your problem.*

\\\

It's clear that this was written too early. May 2005 wasn't the perfect time to get off the merry-go-round; May 2007 was. Being early provided a good reminder about the pain involved in being too far ahead of your time. Having said that, it was much better to get off too soon in May 2005 than to stay on past May 2007.

JOEL GREENBLATT: *High valuations can often go higher and last for longer than expected, continually frustrating disciplined and patient value investors.*

∼

I've tried to make clear that the investment environment greatly influences outcomes. To wring high returns from a low-return environment requires the ability to swim against the tide and find the relatively few winners. This must be based on some combination of exceptional skill, high risk bearing and good luck.

High-return environments, on the other hand, offer opportunities for generous returns through purchases at low prices, and typically these can be earned with low risk. In the crises of 1990, 2002 and 2008, for example, not only did our funds earn unusually high returns, but we feel they did it through investments where loss was unlikely.

The absolute best buying opportunities come when asset holders are forced to sell, and in those crises they were present in large numbers. From time to time, holders become forced sellers for reasons like these:

- The funds they manage experience withdrawals.
- Their portfolio holdings violate investment guidelines such as minimum credit ratings or position maximums.
- They receive margin calls because the value of their assets fails to satisfy requirements agreed to in contracts with their lenders.

PAUL JOHNSON: *Interestingly, although Marks only implies it, investors should work to never put themselves in a position to be a forced seller for these exact reasons.*

As I've said many times, the real goal of active investment management is to buy things for less than they're worth. This is what the efficient market hypothesis says we can't do. The theory's objection seems reasonable: why should someone part with something at a bargain price, especially if the potential seller is informed and rational?

Usually, would-be sellers balance the desire to get a good price with the desire to get the trade done soon. The beauty of forced sellers is that they have no choice. They have a gun at their heads and have to sell regardless of price. Those last three words—*regardless of price*—are the most beautiful in the world if you're on the other side of the transaction.

If a single holder is forced to sell, dozens of buyers will be there to accommodate, so the trade may take place at a price that is only slightly reduced. But if chaos is widespread, many people will be forced to sell at the same time and few people will be in a position to provide the required liquidity. The difficulties that mandate selling—plummeting prices, withdrawal of credit, fear among counterparties or clients—have the same impact on most investors. In that case, prices can fall far below intrinsic value.

The fourth quarter of 2008 provided an excellent example of the need for liquidity in times of chaos. Let's focus on leveraged investment entities' holdings of senior bank loans. Because these loans were highly rated and credit was freely available during the years leading up to the crisis, it was easy to borrow large sums with which to lever debt portfolios, magnifying the potential returns. A typical investor on "margin" might have agreed to post additional capital if the price of the collateral fell below 85 cents on the dollar, secure in the knowledge that in the past, loans like these had never traded much below "par," or 100 cents on the dollar.

When the credit crisis hit, everything went wrong for leveraged investors in bank loans. (And because the yields on these supposedly safe loans had been so low, almost all of the buyers had used leverage to enhance their expected returns.) Loan prices fell. Liquidity dried up. Since much of the buying had been done with borrowed funds, the credit market contraction affected large numbers of holders. As the number of would-be sellers exploded, buyers for cash disappeared. And with additional credit unavailable, no new levered buyers could step forward to absorb the selling.

Prices fell to 95, and then 90, and then 85. And as each portfolio reached its "trigger," the bank issued a margin call, or a demand for a capital infusion. Few investors had the resources and nerve required to add capital in that environment, so the banks took over the portfolios and liquidated them. BWIC, pronounced "bee-wick," came into common use, an acronym for "bid wanted in competition." Investors were informed of a BWIC in the afternoon and told bids were wanted for an auction to be held the next morning. The few possible buyers bid low, hoping to get real bargains (no one needed to worry about bidding too low, since there was sure to be another BWIC behind this one). And the banks weren't concerned with getting fair prices; all they needed was enough proceeds to cover their loans (perhaps 75 or 80 cents on the dollar). Any excess would go to the investor, but the banks didn't care about generating anything for them. Thus BWICs took place at incredibly low prices.

Loan prices eventually fell into the 60s, and every holder on short-term credit who couldn't access additional capital was likely wiped out. Selling prices were ridiculous. The declines on senior loan indices in 2008 exceeded those on subordinated high yield bond indices, certainly signaling an inefficiency. You could buy first lien debt at prices from which you would break even if the issuing company turned out to be worth 20 to 40 percent of what a buyout fund had paid for it just a year or two earlier. The promised yields were very large, and in fact much of this paper appreciated dramatically in 2009.

This was a time for the patient opportunist to step forward. It was primarily those who had been cognizant of the risks in 2006 and 2007 and kept their powder dry—waiting for opportunity—who were able to do so.

The key during a crisis is to be (a) insulated from the forces that require selling and (b) positioned to be a buyer instead.

PAUL JOHNSON: *Although extremely challenging to follow, this is excellent advice.*

To satisfy those criteria, an investor needs the following things: staunch reliance on value, little or no use of leverage, long-term capital and a strong stomach. Patient opportunism, buttressed by a contrarian attitude and a strong balance sheet, can yield amazing profits during meltdowns.

14

The Most Important Thing Is . . .
Knowing What You Don't Know

We have two classes of forecasters: Those who don't
know—and those who don't know they don't know.

JOHN KENNETH GALBRAITH

It's frightening to think that you might not know something, but more frightening to think that, by and large,
the world is run by people who have faith that they know
exactly what's going on.

AMOS TVERSKY

There are two kinds of people who lose money: those
who know nothing and those who know everything.

HENRY KAUFMAN

I've chosen three quotes with which to lead off this chapter, and I have a
million more where those came from. Awareness of the limited extent of
our foreknowledge is an essential component of my approach to investing.

I'm firmly convinced that (a) it's hard to know what the macro future
holds and (b) few people possess superior knowledge of these matters that
can regularly be turned into an investing advantage. There are two caveats, however:

- The more we concentrate on smaller-picture things, the more it's possible to gain a knowledge advantage. With hard work and skill, we can

consistently know more than the next person about individual companies and securities, but that's much less likely with regard to markets and economies. Thus, I suggest people try to "know the knowable."

- An exception comes in the form of my suggestion, on which I elaborate in the next chapter, that investors should make an effort to figure out where they stand at a moment in time in terms of cycles and pendulums. That won't render the future twists and turns knowable, but it can help one prepare for likely developments.

I am not going to try to prove my contention that the future is unknowable. You can't prove a negative, and that certainly includes this one. However, I have yet to meet anyone who consistently knows what lies ahead macro-wise. Of all the economists and strategists you follow, are any correct most of the time?

PAUL JOHNSON: *I can sum up the chapter with the following: Be very careful with your own forecasts and even more careful with those of others! I have found that the message from this chapter is exceedingly important to deliver to students. Most are in their late twenties or early thirties and overconfident in their own abilities, particularly in forecasting the future. No matter how much evidence I present discounting the value of forecasting, most leave school undaunted. I am sure these students are not the only ones that will benefit from Marks's excellent treatment of the impossibility of consistently producing valuable forecasts.*

∼

My "research" on this subject (and I use quotation marks because my efforts in the area are too limited and anecdotal to be considered serious research) has consisted primarily of reading forecasts and observing their lack of utility. I wrote two memos as a result, "The Value of Predictions, or Where'd All This Rain Come From?" (February 15, 1993) and "The Value of Predictions II, or Give That Man a Cigar" (August 22, 1996). In the second memo, I used data from three semiannual *Wall Street Journal* economic polls to examine the usefulness of forecasts.

First, were the forecasts generally accurate? The answer was clearly no. On average, the predictions for the ninety-day T-bill rate, thirty-year bond rate and yen/dollar exchange rate six and twelve months out were off by 15 percent. The average forecaster missed the interest rate on the long bond six months later by 96 basis points (a divergence big enough to change the value of a $1,000 bond by $120).

Second, were the forecasts valuable? Predictions are most useful when they correctly anticipate change. If you predict that something won't change and it doesn't change, that prediction is unlikely to earn you much money. But accurately predicting change can be very profitable. In the *Journal* polls, I observed, the forecasters completely missed several major changes (when accurate forecasts would've helped people make money or avoid a loss): the interest rate increases of 1994 and 1996, the rate decline of 1995 and the massive gyrations of the dollar/yen relationship. In summary, there simply wasn't much correlation between predicted changes and actual changes.

Third, what was the source of the forecasts? The answer here is simple: most of the forecasts consisted of extrapolations. On average, the predictions were within 5 percent of the levels that prevailed at the time they were made. Like many forecasters, these economists were driving with their eyes firmly fixed on the rearview mirror, enabling them to tell us where things were but not where they were going. This bears out the old adage that "it's difficult to make accurate predictions, especially with regard to the future." The corollary is also true: predicting the past is a snap.

Fourth, were the forecasters ever right? The answer is a firm yes. For example, in each semiannual forecast, someone nailed the yield on the thirty-year bond within 10 or 20 basis points, even as interest rates changed radically. The winning forecast was much more accurate than the consensus forecast, which was off by 70 to 130 basis points.

Fifth, if the forecasters were sometimes right—and right so dramatically—then why do I remain so negative on forecasts? Because the important thing in forecasting isn't getting it right once. The important thing is getting it right consistently.

I went on in the 1996 memo to show "two things that might make you think twice about heeding the winners' forecasts." First, they generally failed to make accurate predictions in surveys other than the one they won. And second, half the time in the surveys they didn't win, their forecasts were much more wrong than even the inaccurate consensus. The most important thing, of course, isn't the data, but the conclusions (assuming they're correct and capable of being generalized) and their ramifications.

> One way to get to be right sometimes is to always be bullish or always be bearish; if you hold a fixed view long enough, you may be right sooner or later. And if you're always an outlier, you're likely to eventually be applauded for an extremely unconventional forecast that correctly foresaw what no one else did. But that doesn't mean your forecasts are regularly of any value. . . .
>
> It's possible to be right about the macro-future once in a while, but not on a regular basis. It doesn't do any good to possess a survey of sixty-four forecasts that includes a few that are accurate; you have to know which ones they are. And if the accurate forecasts each six months are made by different economists, it's hard to believe there's much value in the collective forecasts.
>
> "THE VALUE OF PREDICTIONS II, OR GIVE THAT MAN A CIGAR,"
>
> AUGUST 22, 1996

This discussion of forecasts suggests that we have a dilemma: investment results will be determined entirely by what happens in the future, and while we may know what will happen much of the time, when things are "normal," we can't know much about what will happen at those moments when knowing would make the biggest difference.

PAUL JOHNSON: *With this, Marks presents the great investing dilemma.*

- Most of the time, people predict a future that is a lot like the recent past.
- They're not necessarily wrong: most of the time the future largely *is* a rerun of the recent past.
- On the basis of these two points, it's possible to conclude that forecasts will prove accurate much of the time: They'll usually extrapolate recent experience and be right.

- However, the many forecasts that correctly extrapolate past experience are of little value. Just as forecasters usually assume a future that's a lot like the past, so do markets, which usually price in a continuation of recent history. Thus if the future turns out to be like the past, it's unlikely big money will be made, even by those who foresaw correctly that it would.
- Once in a while, however, the future turns out to be very different from the past.
- It's at these times that accurate forecasts would be of great value.
- It's also at these times that forecasts are least likely to be correct.
- Some forecasters may turn out to be correct at these pivotal moments, suggesting that it's possible to correctly forecast key events, but it's unlikely to be the same people consistently.
- The sum of this discussion suggests that, on balance, forecasts are of very little value.

PAUL JOHNSON: *These nine bullets offer the best discussion of the shortcomings of forecasting I have ever read.*

If you need proof, ask yourself how many forecasters correctly predicted the subprime problem, global credit crisis and massive meltdown of 2007–2008. You might be able to think of a few, and you might conclude that their forecasts were valuable. But then ask yourself how many of those few went on to correctly foresee the economic recovery that started slowly in 2009 and the massive market rebound that year. I think the answer's "very few."

And that's not an accident. Those who got 2007–2008 right probably did so at least in part because of a tendency toward negative views. As such, they probably stayed negative for 2009. The overall usefulness of those forecasts wasn't great . . . even though they were partially right about some of the most momentous financial events in the last eighty years.

So the key question isn't "are forecasters sometimes right?" but rather "are forecasts as a whole—or any one person's forecasts—consistently actionable and valuable?" No one should bet much on the answer being affirmative.

A prediction of global crisis in 2007–2008 would have had great potential value. But if you saw that it came from someone who wasn't right consistently—and someone with a visible negative bias—would you have acted? That's the trouble with inconsistent forecasters: not that they're never right, but that the record isn't positive enough to inspire action on their occasional brainstorms.

~

It's no secret that I have a limited opinion of forecasters and those who resolutely believe in them. In fact, I've come up with a label for these people.

Most of the investors I've met over the years have belonged to the "I know" school. It's easy to identify them.

- They think knowledge of the future direction of economies, interest rates, markets and widely followed mainstream stocks is essential for investment success.
- They're confident it can be achieved.
- They know they can do it.
- They're aware that lots of other people are trying to do it too, but they figure either (a) everyone can be successful at the same time, or (b) only a few can be, but they're among them.
- They're comfortable investing based on their opinions regarding the future.
- They're also glad to share their views with others, even though correct forecasts should be of such great value that no one would give them away gratis.
- They rarely look back to rigorously assess their record as forecasters.

///

PAUL JOHNSON: *Human beings are prone to want to make forecasts (it appears to be part of our natural wiring), and I suspect no amount of evidence is going to stop most from doing just that. However, Marks suggests that at the very least one should keep one's own forecasting track record.*

\\\

Confident is the key word for describing members of this school. For the "I don't know" school, on the other hand, the word—especially when dealing with the macro-future—is *guarded*. Its adherents generally believe you can't know the future; you don't have to know the future; and the proper goal is to do the best possible job of investing in the absence of that knowledge.

As a member of the "I know" school, you get to opine on the future (and maybe have people take notes). You may be sought out for your opinions and considered a desirable dinner guest . . . especially when the stock market's going up.

Join the "I don't know" school and the results are more mixed. You'll soon tire of saying "I don't know" to friends and strangers alike. After a while, even relatives will stop asking where you think the market's going. You'll never get to enjoy that one-in-a-thousand moment when your forecast comes true and the *Wall Street Journal* runs your picture. On the other hand, you'll be spared all those times when forecasts miss the mark, as well as the losses that can result from investing based on overrated knowledge of the future.

"US AND THEM," MAY 7, 2004

No one likes having to invest for the future under the assumption that the future is largely unknowable.

PAUL JOHNSON: *Here, Marks offers the ultimate investing challenge and one of the key drivers of the desire to continue making forecasts.*

On the other hand, if it is, we'd better face up to it and find other ways to cope than through forecasts. Whatever limitations are imposed on us in the investment world, it's a heck of a lot better to acknowledge them and accommodate than to deny them and forge ahead.

Oh yes; one other thing: the biggest problems tend to arise when investors forget about the difference between probability and outcome—that is, when they forget about the limits on foreknowledge:

- when they believe the shape of the probability distribution is knowable with certainty (and that they know it),

- when they assume the most likely outcome is the one that will happen,
- when they assume the expected result accurately represents the actual result, or
- perhaps most important, when they ignore the possibility of improbable outcomes.

HOWARD MARKS: *Understanding uncertainty: Risk and uncertainty aren't the same as loss, but they create the potential for loss when things go wrong. Some of the biggest losses occur when overconfidence regarding predictive ability causes investors to underestimate the range of possibilities, the difficulty of predicting which one will materialize, and the consequences of a surprise.*

Imprudent investors who overlook these limitations tend to make mistakes in their portfolios and experience occasional large losses. That was the story of 2004–2007: because many people overestimated the extent to which outcomes were knowable and controllable, they underestimated the risk present in the things they were doing.

～

The question of whether trying to predict the future will or will not work isn't a matter of idle curiosity or academic musing. It has—or should have—significant ramifications for investor behavior. If you're engaged in an activity that involves decisions with consequences in the future, it seems patently obvious that you'll act one way if you think the future can be foreseen and a very different way if you think it can't.

One key question investors have to answer is whether they view the future as knowable or unknowable. Investors who feel they know what the future holds will act assertively: making directional bets, concentrating positions, levering holdings and counting on future growth—in other words, doing things that in the absence of foreknowledge would increase risk. On the other hand, those who feel they don't know what the future holds will act quite differently: diversifying, hedging, levering less (or not at all), emphasizing value today over growth tomorrow, staying high in the capital structure, and generally girding for a variety of possible outcomes.

The first group of investors did much better in the years leading up to the crash. But the second group was better prepared when the crash unfolded, and they had more capital available (and more-intact psyches) with which to profit from purchases made at its nadir.

"TOUCHSTONES," NOVEMBER 10, 2009

If you know the future, it's silly to play defense. You should behave aggressively and target the greatest winners; there can be no loss to fear. Diversification is unnecessary, and maximum leverage can be employed. In fact, being unduly modest about what you know can result in opportunity costs (forgone profits).

On the other hand, if you don't know what the future holds, it's foolhardy to act as if you do. Harkening back to Amos Tversky and the powerful quote that opened this chapter, the bottom line is clear. Investing in an unknowable future as an agnostic is a daunting prospect, but if foreknowledge is elusive, investing as if you know what's coming is close to nuts. Maybe Mark Twain put it best: "It ain't what you don't know that gets you into trouble. It's what you know for sure that just ain't so."

Overestimating what you're capable of knowing or doing can be extremely dangerous—in brain surgery, transocean racing or investing. Acknowledging the boundaries of what you can know—and working within those limits rather than venturing beyond—can give you a great advantage.

15

The Most Important Thing Is . . .
Having a Sense for Where We Stand

We may never know where we're going, but we'd better
have a good idea where we are.

Market cycles present the investor with a daunting challenge, given that:

- Their ups and downs are inevitable.
- They will profoundly influence our performance as investors.
- They are unpredictable as to extent and, especially, timing.

So we have to cope with a force that will have great impact but is largely unknowable. What, then, are we to do about cycles? The question is of vital importance, but the obvious answers—as so often—are not the right ones.

The first possibility is that rather than accept that cycles are unpredictable, we should redouble our efforts to predict the future, throwing added resources into the battle and betting increasingly on our conclusions. But a great deal of data, and all my experience, tell me that the only thing we can predict about cycles is their inevitability. Further, superior results in investing come from knowing more than others, and it hasn't been demonstrated to my satisfaction that a lot of people know more than the consensus about the timing and extent of future cycles.

The second possibility is to accept that the future isn't knowable, throw up our hands, and simply ignore cycles. Instead of trying to predict them, we could try to make good investments and hold them throughout.

Since we can't know when to hold more or less of them, or when our in-vestment posture should become more aggressive or more defensive, we could simply invest with total disregard for cycles and their profound effect. This is the so-called buy-and-hold approach.

There's a third possibility, however, and in my opinion it's the right one by a wide margin. Why not simply try to figure out where we stand in terms of each cycle and what that implies for our actions?

> In the world of investing, . . . nothing is as dependable as cycles. Fundamentals, psychology, prices and returns will rise and fall, presenting opportunities to make mistakes or to profit from the mistakes of others. They are the givens.
>
> We cannot know how far a trend will go, when it will turn, what will make it turn or how far things will then go in the oppo-site direction. But I'm confident that every trend will stop sooner or later. Nothing goes on forever.
>
> So what can we do about cycles? If we can't know in advance how and when the turns will occur, how can we cope? On this, I am dogmatic: We may never know where we're going, but we'd better have a good idea where we are. That is, even if we can't predict the timing and extent of cyclical fluctuations, it's essential that we strive to ascertain where we stand in cyclical terms and act accordingly.
>
> "IT IS WHAT IT IS," MARCH 27, 2006

PAUL JOHNSON: *I respect Marks's position on this issue. How-ever, this goal is not nearly as simple as he suggests. He does offer a reasonable compromise in the memo below that I found very operational.*

~

It would be wonderful to be able to successfully predict the swings of the pendulum and always move in the appropriate direction, but this is certainly an unrealistic expectation. I consider it far more reasonable to try to (a) stay alert for occasions when a market has reached an extreme, (b) adjust our behavior in response and,

(c) most important, refuse to fall into line with the herd behavior that renders so many investors dead wrong at tops and bottoms.

"FIRST QUARTER PERFORMANCE," APRIL 11, 1991

I don't mean to suggest that if we can figure out where we stand in a cycle we'll know precisely what's coming next. But I do think that understanding will give us valuable insight into future events and what we might do about them, and that's all we can hope for.

∼

When I say that our present position (unlike the future) is knowable, I don't mean to imply that understanding comes automatically. Like most things about investing, it takes work. But it can be done. Here are a few concepts I consider essential in that effort.

First, we must be alert to what's going on. The philosopher Santayana said, "Those who cannot remember the past are condemned to repeat it." In very much the same way, I believe those who are unaware of what's going on around them are destined to be buffeted by it.

As difficult as it is know the future, it's really not that hard to understand the present. What we need to do is "take the market's temperature." If we are alert and perceptive, we can gauge the behavior of those around us and from that judge what we should do.

The essential ingredient here is *inference*, one of my favorite words. Everyone sees what happens each day, as reported in the media. But how many people make an effort to understand what those everyday events say about the psyches of market participants, the investment climate, and thus what we should do in response?

Simply put, we must strive to understand the implications of what's going on around us. When others are recklessly confident and buying aggressively, we should be highly cautious; when others are frightened into inaction or panic selling, we should become aggressive.

So look around, and ask yourself: Are investors optimistic or pessimistic? Do the media talking heads say the markets should be piled into or avoided? Are novel investment schemes readily accepted or dismissed out of hand? Are securities offerings and fund openings being treated as opportunities to get rich or possible pitfalls? Has the credit cycle rendered capital readily available or impossible to obtain? Are price/

earnings ratios high or low in the context of history, and are yield spreads tight or generous?

PAUL JOHNSON: *These insightful questions can easily act as a checklist that investors could use periodically to take the market's temperature.*

All of these things are important, and yet none of them entails forecasting. We can make excellent investment decisions on the basis of present observations, with no need to make guesses about the future.

The key is to take note of things like these and let them tell you what to do. While the markets don't cry out for action along these lines every day, they do at the extremes, when their pronouncements are highly important.

~

The years 2007–2008 can be viewed as a painful time for markets and their participants, or as the greatest learning experience in our lifetimes. They were both, of course, but dwelling on the former isn't of much help. Understanding the latter can make anyone a better investor. I can think of no better example than the devastating credit crisis to illustrate the importance of making accurate observations regarding the present and the folly of trying to forecast the future. It warrants a detailed discussion.

It's obvious in retrospect that the period leading up to the onset of the financial crisis in mid-2007 was one of unbridled—and unconscious— risk taking. With attitudes cool toward stocks and bonds, money flowed to "alternative investments" such as private equity—buyouts—in amounts sufficient to doom them to failure. There was unquestioning acceptance of the proposition that homes and other real estate would provide sure profits and cushion against inflation. And too-free access to capital with low interest rates and loose terms encouraged the use of leverage in amounts that proved excessive.

After-the-fact risk awareness doesn't do much good. The question is whether alertness and inference would have helped one avoid the full brunt of the 2007–2008 market declines. Here are some of the indicators of heatedness we saw:

- The issuance of high yield bonds and below investment grade leveraged loans was at levels that constituted records by wide margins.
- An unusually high percentage of the high yield bond issuance was rated triple-C, a quality level at which new bonds usually can't be sold in large amounts.
- Issuance of debt to raise money for dividends to owners was routine. In normal times, such transactions, which increase the issuers' riskiness and do nothing for creditors, are harder to accomplish.
- Debt was increasingly issued with coupons that could be paid with more debt, and with few or no covenants to protect creditors.
- Formerly rare triple-A debt ratings were assigned by the thousands to tranches of untested structured vehicles.
- Buyouts were done at increasing multiples of cash flow and at increasing leverage ratios. On average, buyout firms paid 50 percent more for a dollar of cash flow in 2007 than they had in 2001.
- There were buyouts of firms in highly cyclical industries such as semiconductor manufacturing. In more skeptical times, investors take a dim view of combining leverage and cyclicality.

Taking all these things into consideration, a clear inference was possible: that providers of capital were competing to do so, easing terms and interest rates rather than demanding adequate protection and potential rewards. The seven scariest words in the world for the thoughtful investor—*too much money chasing too few deals*—provided an unusually apt description of market conditions.

HOWARD MARKS: *The riskiest things: When buyers compete to put large amounts of capital to work in a market, prices are bid up relative to value, prospective returns shrink, and risk rises. It's only when buyers predominate relative to sellers that you can have highly overpriced assets. The warning signs shouldn't be hard to spot.*

You can tell when too much money is competing to be deployed. The number of deals being done increases, as does the ease of doing deals; the cost of capital declines; and the price for the asset being bought rises with each successive transaction. A torrent of capital is what makes it all happen.

If you make cars and want to sell more of them over the long term—
that is, take permanent market share from your competitors—
you'll try to make your product better. . . . That's why—one way or
the other—most sales pitches say, "Ours is better." However, there
are products that can't be differentiated, and economists call them
"commodities." They're goods where no seller's offering is much
different from any other. They tend to trade on price alone, and
each buyer is likely to take the offering at the lowest delivered
price. Thus, if you deal in a commodity and want to sell more of it,
there's generally one way to do so: cut your price. . . .

It helps to think of money as a commodity just like those
others. Everyone's money is pretty much the same. Yet institutions seeking to add to loan volume, and private equity funds and
hedge funds seeking to increase their fees, all want to move more
of it. So if you want to place more money—that is, get people to go
to you instead of your competitors for their financing—you have
to make your money cheaper.

One way to lower the price for your money is by reducing the
interest rate you charge on loans. A slightly more subtle way is
to agree to a higher price for the thing you're buying, such as by
paying a higher price/earnings ratio for a common stock or a
higher total transaction price when you're buying a company. Any
way you slice it, you're settling for a lower prospective return.

"THE RACE TO THE BOTTOM," FEBRUARY 17, 2007

One trend investors might have observed during this dangerous period, had they been alert, was the movement along the spectrum that runs
from skepticism to credulousness in regard to what I described earlier as
the silver bullet or can't-lose investment. Thoughtful investors might
have noticed that the appetite for silver bullets was running high, meaning greed had won out over fear and signifying a nonskeptical—and thus
risky—market.

Hedge funds came to be viewed as just such a sure thing during the
last decade, and especially those called "absolute return" funds. These were
long/short or arbitrage funds that wouldn't pursue high returns by making "directional" bets on the market's trend. Rather, the managers' skill or
technology would enable them to produce consistent returns in the range
of 8 to 11 percent regardless of which way the market went.

Too few people recognized that achieving rock-steady returns in that range would be a phenomenal accomplishment—perhaps too good to be true. (N.B.: that's exactly what Bernard Madoff purported to be earning.) Too few wondered (a) how many managers there are with enough talent to produce that miracle, especially after the deduction of substantial management and incentive fees, (b) how much money they could do it with and (c) how their highly levered bets on small statistical discrepancies would fare in a hostile environment. (In the difficult year of 2008, the term *absolute return* was shown to have been overused and misused, as the average fund lost about 18 percent.)

As described at length in chapter 6, we heard at the time that risk had been eliminated through the newly popular wonders of securitization, tranching, selling onward, disintermediation and decoupling. Tranching deserves particular attention here. It consists of allocating a portfolio's value and cash flow to stakeholders in various tiers of seniority. The owners of the top-tier claim get paid first; thus, they enjoy the greatest safety and settle for relatively low returns. Those with bottom-tier claims are in the "first-loss" position, and in exchange for accepting heightened risk they enjoy the potential for high returns from the residual that's left over after the fixed claims of the senior tranches have been paid off.

In the years 2004–2007, the notion arose that if you cut risk into small pieces and sell the pieces off to investors best suited to hold them, the risk disappears. Sounds like magic. Thus, it's no coincidence that the tranched securitizations from which so much was expected became the site of many of the worst meltdowns: there's simply no magic in investing.

Absolute return funds, low-cost leverage, riskless real estate investments and tranched debt vehicles were all the rage. Of course, the error in all these things became clear beginning in August 2007. It turned out that risk hadn't been banished and, in fact, had been elevated by investors' excessive trust and insufficient skepticism.

The period from 2004 through the middle of 2007 presented investors with one of the greatest opportunities to outperform by reducing their risk, if only they were perceptive enough to recognize what was going on and confident enough to act. All you really had to do was take the market's temperature during an overheated period and deplane as it continued upward. Those who were able to do so exemplify the principles of contrarianism, discussed in chapter 11. Contrarian investors who had cut their risk and otherwise prepared during the lead-up to the crisis lost less in the

2008 meltdown and were best positioned to take advantage of the vast bargains it created.

∽

There are few fields in which decisions as to strategies and tactics aren't influenced by what we see in the environment. Our pressure on the gas pedal varies depending on whether the road is empty or crowded. The golfer's choice of club depends on the wind. Our decision regarding outerwear certainly varies with the weather. Shouldn't our investment actions be equally affected by the investing climate?

Most people strive to adjust their portfolios based on what they think lies ahead. At the same time, however, most people would admit forward visibility just isn't that great. That's why I make the case for responding to the current realities and their implications, as opposed to expecting the future to be made clear.

"IT IS WHAT IT IS," MARCH 27, 2006

∽

THE POOR MAN'S GUIDE TO MARKET ASSESSMENT

Here's a simple exercise that might help you take the temperature of future markets. I have listed a number of market characteristics. For each pair, check off the one you think is most descriptive of today. And if you find that most of your checkmarks are in the left-hand column, as I do, hold on to your wallet.

Economy:	Vibrant	Sluggish
Outlook:	Positive	Negative
Lenders:	Eager	Reticent
Capital markets:	Loose	Tight
Capital:	Plentiful	Scarce
Terms:	Easy	Restrictive
Interest rates:	Low	High
Spreads:	Narrow	Wide

Investors:	Optimistic	Pessimistic
	Sanguine	Distressed
	Eager to buy	Uninterested in buying
Asset owners:	Happy to hold	Rushing for the exits
Sellers:	Few	Many
Markets:	Crowded	Starved for attention
Funds:	Hard to gain entry	Open to anyone
	New ones daily	Only the best can raise money
	General Partners hold all the cards	Limited Partners have bargaining power
Recent performance:	Strong	Weak
Asset prices:	High	Low
Prospective returns:	Low	High
Risk:	High	Low
Popular qualities:	Aggressiveness	Caution and discipline
	Broad reach	Selectivity

"IT IS WHAT IT IS," MARCH 27, 2006

CHRISTOPHER DAVIS: *This table might be even more useful if it would allow for scaling—i.e., use a 1 to 5 scale for each category and allow "N/As" where necessary. With that modification, this is a great guide.*

JOEL GREENBLATT: *A wonderful chart and a great exercise.*

PAUL JOHNSON: *I feel strongly that running through this checklist twice a year would allow an investor to keep tabs on the swing of the market's pendulum. After a decade, the investor would have a rich database of past market swings from which to draw. I wish I had started such a list ten years ago.*

~

Markets move cyclically, rising and falling. The pendulum oscillates, rarely pausing at the "happy medium," the midpoint of its arc. Is this a source of danger or of opportunity? And what are investors to do about it? My response is simple: try to figure out what's going on around us, and use that to guide our actions.

16

The Most Important Thing Is . . .
Appreciating the Role of Luck

Every once in a while, someone makes a risky bet on an improbable or uncertain outcome and ends up looking like a genius. But we should recognize that it happened because of luck and boldness, not skill.

The investment world is not an orderly and logical place where the future can be predicted and specific actions always produce specific results. The truth is, much in investing is ruled by luck. Some may prefer to call it *chance* or *randomness*, and those words do sound more sophisticated than *luck*. But it comes down to the same thing: a great deal of the success of everything we do as investors will be heavily influenced by the roll of the dice.

PAUL JOHNSON: *For me the theme of this chapter is: Learn to be honest with yourself about your successes and failures. Learn to recognize the role luck has played in all outcomes. Learn to decide which outcomes came about because of skill and which because of luck. Until one learns to identify the true source of success, one will be fooled by randomness.*

To fully explore the notion of luck, in this chapter I want to advance some ideas expressed by Nassim Nicholas Taleb in his book *Fooled by Randomness*. Some of the concepts I explore here occurred to me before I read it, but Taleb's book put it all together for me and added more. I consider it one of the most important books an investor can read.

PAUL JOHNSON: *I, too, am a huge fan of Nassim Taleb's work, much of which Marks draws on for this chapter. I am particularly fond of Taleb's concept of alternative histories, and Marks does an excellent job of incorporating this concept into his investment philosophy.*

I borrowed some of Taleb's ideas for a 2002 memo titled "Returns and How They Get That Way," which incorporated excerpts from *Fooled by Randomness*, represented here by italics.

Randomness (or luck) plays a huge part in life's results, and outcomes that hinge on random events should be viewed as different from those that do not.

Thus, when considering whether an investment record is likely to be repeated, it is essential to think about the role of randomness in the manager's results, and whether the performance resulted from skill or simply being lucky.

> *$10 million earned through Russian roulette does not have the same value as $10 million earned through the diligent and artful practice of dentistry. They are the same, can buy the same goods, except that one's dependence on randomness is greater than the other. To your accountant, though, they would be identical. . . . Yet, deep down, I cannot help but consider them as qualitatively different.*

Every record should be considered in light of the other outcomes—Taleb calls them "alternative histories"—that could have occurred just as easily as the "visible histories" that did.

> *Clearly my way of judging matters is probabilistic in nature; it relies on the notion of what could have probably happened. . . .*
> *If we have heard of [history's great generals and inventors], it is simply because they took considerable risks, along with thousands of others, and happened to win. They were intelligent, courageous, noble (at times), had the highest possible obtainable*

culture in their day—but so did thousands of others who live in
the musty footnotes of history.

Every once in a while, someone makes a risky bet on an improbable or uncertain outcome and ends up looking like a genius.
But we should recognize that it happened because of luck and
boldness, not skill.

Think about the aggressive backgammon player who can't
win without a roll of double sixes, with its probability of happening once in every thirty-six rolls of the dice. The player accepts
the cube—doubling the stakes—and then gets his boxcars. It
might have been an unwise bet, but because it succeeded, everybody considers the player brilliant. We should think about how
probable it was that something other than double sixes would
materialize, and thus how lucky the player was to have won. This
says a lot about the player's likelihood of winning again. . . .

In the short run, a great deal of investment success can result
from just being in the right place at the right time. I always say the
keys to profit are aggressiveness, timing and skill, and someone who
has enough aggressiveness at the right time doesn't need much skill.

At a given time in the markets, the most profitable traders are
likely to be those that are best fit to the latest cycle. This does not
happen too often with dentists or pianists—because of the na-
ture of randomness.

The easy way to see this is that in boom times, the highest
returns often go to those who take the most risk. That doesn't say
anything about their being the best investors.

Warren Buffett's appendix to the fourth revised edition of
The Intelligent Investor describes a contest in which each of the 225
million Americans starts with $1 and flips a coin once a day. The
people who get it right on day one collect a dollar from those who
were wrong and go on to flip again on day two, and so forth. Ten
days later, 220,000 people have called it right ten times in a row
and won $1,000. "They may try to be modest, but at cocktail par-
ties they will occasionally admit to attractive members of the opposite sex what their technique is, and what marvelous insights
they bring to the field of flipping." After another ten days, we're

down to 215 survivors who've been right 20 times in a row and have each won $1 million. They write books titled like *How I Turned a Dollar into a Million in Twenty Days Working Thirty Seconds a Morning* and sell tickets to seminars. Sound familiar?

Thus, randomness contributes to (or wrecks) investment records to a degree that few people appreciate fully. As a result, the dangers that lurk in thus-far-successful strategies often are underrated.

Perhaps a good way to sum up Taleb's views is by excerpting from a table in his book. He lists in the first column a number of things that easily can be mistaken for the things in the second column.

Luck	*Skill*
Randomness	*Determinism*
Probability	*Certainty*
Belief, conjecture	*Knowledge, certitude*
Theory	*Reality*
Anecdote, coincidence	*Causality, law*
Survivorship bias	*Market outperformance*
Lucky idiot	*Skilled investor*

I think this dichotomization is sheer brilliance. We all know that when things go right, luck looks like skill. Coincidence looks like causality. A "lucky idiot" looks like a skilled investor. Of course, knowing that randomness can have this effect doesn't make it easy to distinguish between lucky investors and skillful investors.

//

SETH KLARMAN: *This is why it is all-important to look not at investors' track records but at what they are doing to achieve those records. Does it make sense? Does it appear replicable? Why haven't competitive forces priced away any apparent market inefficiencies that enabled this investment success?*

**

But we must keep trying.

I find that I agree with essentially all of Taleb's important points.

- Investors are right (and wrong) all the time for the "wrong reason." Someone buys a stock because he or she expects a certain development; it doesn't occur; the market takes the stock up anyway; the investor looks good (and invariably accepts credit).
- The correctness of a decision can't be judged from the outcome. Nevertheless, that's how people assess it. A good decision is one that's optimal at the time it's made, when the future is by definition unknown. Thus, correct decisions are often unsuccessful, and vice versa.
- Randomness alone can produce just about any outcome in the short run. In portfolios that are allowed to reflect them fully, market movements can easily swamp the skillfulness of the manager (or lack thereof). But certainly market movements cannot be credited to the manager (unless he or she is the rare market timer who's capable of getting it right repeatedly).
- For these reasons, investors often receive credit they don't deserve. One good coup can be enough to build a reputation, but clearly a coup can arise out of randomness alone. Few of these "geniuses" are right more than once or twice in a row.
- Thus, it's essential to have a large number of observations—lots of years of data—before judging a given manager's ability.

"RETURNS AND HOW THEY GET THAT WAY,"

NOVEMBER 11, 2002

～

Taleb's idea of "alternative histories"—the other things that reasonably could have happened—is a fascinating concept, and one that is particularly relevant to investing.

Most people acknowledge the uncertainty that surrounds the future, but they feel that at least the past is known and fixed. After all, the past is history, absolute and unchanging. But Taleb points out that the things that happened are only a small subset of the things that *could* have happened. Thus, the fact that a stratagem or action worked—under the circumstances that unfolded—doesn't necessarily prove the decision behind it was wise.

Maybe what ultimately made the decision a success was a completely unlikely event, something that was just a matter of luck. In that case that decision—as successful as it turned out to be—may have been unwise, and the many other histories that could have happened would have shown the error of the decision.

How much credit should a decision maker receive for having bet on a highly uncertain outcome that unfolded luckily? This is a good question, and it deserves to be looked at in depth.

One of the first things I remember learning after entering Wharton in 1963 was that the quality of a decision is not determined by the outcome. The events that transpire afterward make decisions successful or unsuccessful, and those events are often well beyond anticipating. This idea was powerfully reinforced when I read Taleb's book. He highlights the ability of chance occurrences to reward unwise decisions and penalize good ones.

What is a good decision? Let's say someone decides to build a ski resort in Miami, and three months later a freak blizzard hits south Florida, dumping twelve feet of snow. In its first season, the ski area turns a hefty profit. Does that mean building it was a good decision? No.

A good decision is one that a logical, intelligent and informed person would have made under the circumstances *as they appeared at the time, before the outcome was known.* By that standard, the Miami ski resort looks like folly.

As with risk of loss, many things that will bear on the correctness of a decision cannot be known or quantified in advance. Even after the fact, it can be hard to be sure who made a good decision based on solid analysis but was penalized by a freak occurrence, and who benefited from taking a flier. Thus, it can be hard to know who made the best decision. On the other hand, past returns are easily assessed, making it easy to know who made the most *profitable* decision. It's easy to confuse the two, but insightful investors must be highly conscious of the difference.

HOWARD MARKS: *Fear of looking wrong: It's counterintuitive but extremely important: given the randomness and variability at work in our environment, it's often true that good decisions fail to work and bad decisions succeed. In particular, investors are "right for the wrong reason" (and vice versa) all the time. You mustn't let this frustrate you and convince you your good decisions were mistakes (unless so many prove wrong that you have to consider that possibility).*

In the long run, there's no reasonable alternative to believing that good decisions will lead to investment profits. In the short run, however, we must be stoic when they don't.

PAUL JOHNSON: *I love this observation. Oh so very true!*

~

Since the investors of the "I know" school, described in chapter 14, feel it's possible to know the future, they decide what it will look like, build portfolios designed to maximize returns under that one scenario, and largely disregard the other possibilities. The suboptimizers of the "I don't know" school, on the other hand, put their emphasis on constructing portfolios that will do well in the scenarios they consider likely and not too poorly in the rest.

Investors who belong to the "I know" school predict how the dice will come up, attribute their successes to their astute sense of the future, and blame bad luck when things don't go their way. When they're right, the question that has to be asked is "Could they really have seen the future or couldn't they?" Because their approach is probabilistic, investors of the "I don't know" school understand that the outcome is largely up to the gods, and thus that the credit or blame accorded the investors—especially in the short run—should be appropriately limited.

The "I know" school quickly and confidently divides its members into winners and losers based on the first roll or two of the dice. Investors of the "I don't know" school understand that their skill should be judged over a large number of rolls, not just one (and that rolls can be few and far between). Thus they accept that their cautious, suboptimzing approach may produce undistinguished results for a while, but they're confident that if they're superior investors, that will be apparent in the long run.

Short-term gains and short-term losses are potential impostors, as neither is necessarily indicative of real investment ability (or the lack thereof).

PAUL JOHNSON: *This is a great line. How many investors have fallen for this mistake?*

Surprisingly good returns are often just the flip side of surprisingly bad returns. One year with a great return can overstate the manager's skill and obscure the risk he or she took. Yet people are surprised when that great year is followed by a terrible year. Investors invariably lose track of the fact that both short-term gains and short-term losses can be impostors, and of the importance of digging deep to understand what underlies them.

Investment performance is what happens to a portfolio when events unfold. People pay great heed to the resulting performance, but the questions they should ask are, Were the events that unfolded (and the other possibilities that didn't unfold) truly within the ken of the portfolio manager? And what would the performance have been if other events had occurred instead? Those other events are Taleb's "alternative histories."

"PIGWEED," DECEMBER 7, 2006

JOEL GREENBLATT: *The best-performing mutual fund for the decade of the 2000s made 18 percent per year. The average (dollar-weighted) investor in the fund lost 8 percent per year during this same period. Investment inflows followed "up" performance, or outperformance and outflows followed losses or underperformance. Apparently, there was little long-term assessment of investment skill by most investors when making allocation decisions.*

I find Taleb's ideas novel and provocative. Once you realize the vast extent to which randomness can affect investment outcomes, you look at everything in a very different light.

The actions of the "I know" school are based on a view of a single future that is knowable and conquerable. My "I don't know" school thinks of future events in terms of a probability distribution. That's a big difference. In the latter case, we may have an idea which one outcome is most likely to occur, but we also know there are many other possibilities, and those other outcomes may have a collective likelihood much higher than the one we consider most likely.

HOWARD MARKS: *Understanding uncertainty: People who think the future is knowable (and that they can know it) belong to what I call the "I know" school. They ignore the presence of uncertainty and act in ways that will increase profits if they're right but expose them to increased losses if they're wrong. Recognizing this, it's important for all investors to figure out whether they know and act accordingly.*

Clearly, Taleb's view of an uncertain world is much more consistent with mine. Everything I believe and recommend about investing proceeds from that school of thought.

- We should spend our time trying to find value among the knowable— industries, companies and securities—rather than base our decisions on what we expect from the less-knowable macro world of economies and broad market performance.
- Given that we don't know exactly which future will obtain, we have to get value on our side by having a strongly held, analytically derived opinion of it and buying for less when opportunities to do so present themselves.
- We have to practice defensive investing, since many of the outcomes are likely to go against us. It's more important to ensure survival under negative outcomes than it is to guarantee maximum returns under favorable ones.
- To improve our chances of success, we have to emphasize acting contrary to the herd when it's at extremes, being aggressive when the market is low and cautious when it's high.
- Given the highly indeterminate nature of outcomes, we must view strategies and their results—both good and bad—with suspicion until proved out over a large number of trials.

CHRISTOPHER DAVIS: *This is a very good summary.*

Several things go together for those who view the world as an uncertain place: healthy respect for risk; awareness that we don't know what the future holds; an understanding that the best we can do is view the future as a probability distribution and invest accordingly; insistence on defensive investing; and emphasis on avoiding pitfalls.

JOEL GREENBLATT: *For good investors, as the time horizon expands, which allows skill to come into play, the probability distribution of long-term returns should narrow.*

To me that's what thoughtful investing is all about.

17

The Most Important Thing Is . . .
Investing Defensively

There are old investors, and there are bold investors, but there are no old bold investors.

JOEL GREENBLATT: *This saying works double for old pilots and bold pilots.*

When friends ask me for personal investment advice, my first step is to try to understand their attitude toward risk and return. Asking for investment advice without specifying that is like asking a doctor for a good medicine without telling him or her what ails you.

So I ask, "Which do you care about more, making money or avoiding losses?" The answer is invariably the same: both.

The problem is that you can't simultaneously go all out for both profit making and loss avoidance. Each investor has to take a position regarding these two goals, and usually that requires striking a reasonable balance. The decision should be made consciously and rationally. This chapter's about the choice . . . and my recommendation.

The best way to put this decision into perspective is by thinking of it in terms of offense versus defense. And one of the best ways to consider this is through the metaphor of sports.

To establish the groundwork for this discussion, I'll refer to the wonderful article by Charles Ellis, titled "The Loser's Game," that appeared in *The Financial Analysts Journal* in 1975. This may have been my first exposure to a direct analogy between investing and sports, and it was absolutely seminal regarding my emphasis on defensive investing.

Charley's article described the perceptive analysis of tennis contained in *Extraordinary Tennis for the Ordinary Tennis Player* by Dr. Simon Ramo, the "R" in TRW, once a conglomerate with products ranging from auto parts to credit reporting services. Ramo pointed out that professional tennis is a "winner's game," in which the match goes to the player who's able to hit the most winners: fast-paced, well-placed shots that an opponent can't return.

Given anything other than an outright winner by an opponent, professional tennis players can make the shot they want almost all the time: hard or soft, deep or short, left or right, flat or with spin. Professional players aren't troubled by the things that make the game challenging for amateurs: bad bounces; wind; sun in the eyes; limitations on speed, stamina and skill; or an opponent's efforts to put the ball beyond reach. The pros can get to most shots their opponents hit and do what they want with the ball almost all the time. In fact, pros can do this so consistently that tennis statisticians keep track of the relatively rare exceptions under the heading "unforced errors."

But the tennis the rest of us play is a "loser's game," with the match going to the player who hits the fewest losers. The winner just keeps the ball in play until the loser hits it into the net or off the court. In other words, in amateur tennis, points aren't won; they're lost. I recognized in Ramo's loss-avoidance strategy the version of tennis I try to play.

Charley Ellis took Ramo's idea a step further, applying it to investments. His views on market efficiency and the high cost of trading led him to conclude that the pursuit of winners in the mainstream stock markets is unlikely to pay off for the investor. Instead, you should try to avoid hitting losers. I found this view of investing absolutely compelling.

The choice between offense and defense investing should be based on how much the investor believes is within his or her control. In my view, investing entails a lot that isn't.

Professional tennis players can be quite sure that if they do A, B, C and D with their feet, body, arms and racquet, the ball will do E just about every time; there are relatively few random variables at work. But investing is full of bad bounces and unanticipated developments, and the dimensions of the court and the height of the net change all the time. The workings of economies and markets are highly imprecise and variable, and the thinking and behavior of the other players constantly alter the environment. Even if you do everything right, other investors can ignore your favorite stock; management can squander the company's opportunities; government can change the rules; or nature can serve up a catastrophe.

So much is within the control of professional tennis players that they really should go for winners. And they'd better, since if they serve up easy balls, their opponents will hit winners of their own and take points. In contrast, investment results are only partly within the investors' control, and investors can make good money—and outlast their opponents—without trying tough shots.

The bottom line is that even highly skilled investors can be guilty of mis-hits, and the overaggressive shot can easily lose them the match. Thus, defense—significant emphasis on keeping things from going wrong—is an important part of every great investor's game.

∾

There are a lot of things I like about investing, and most of them are true of sports as well.

- *It's competitive*—some succeed and some fail, and the distinction is clear.
- *It's quantitative*—you can see the results in black and white.
- *It's a meritocracy*—in the long term, the better returns go to the superior investors.
- *It's team oriented*—an effective group can accomplish more than one person.
- *It's satisfying and enjoyable*—but much more so when you win.

These positives can make investing a very rewarding activity in which to engage. But as in sports, there are also negatives.

- There can be a premium on aggressiveness, which doesn't serve well in the long run.
- Unlucky bounces can be frustrating.
- Short-term success can lead to widespread recognition without enough attention being paid to the likely durability and consistency of the record.

Overall, I think investing and sports are quite similar, and so are the decisions they call for.

Think about an American football game. The offense has the ball. They have four tries to make ten yards. If they don't, the referee blows the whistle. The clock stops. Off the field goes the offense and on comes the defense, whose job it is to stop the other team from advancing the ball.

Is football a good metaphor for your view of investing? Well, I'll tell you, it isn't for mine. In investing there's no one there to blow the whistle; you rarely know when to switch from offense to defense; and there aren't any time-outs during which to do it.

No, I think investing is more like the "football" that's played outside the United States—soccer. In soccer, the same eleven players are on the field for essentially the whole game. There isn't an offensive squad and a defensive squad. The same people have to play both ways ... have to be able to deal with all eventualities. Collectively, those eleven players must have the potential to score goals and stop the opposition from scoring more.

A soccer coach has to decide whether to field a team that emphasizes offense (in order to score a lot of goals and somehow hold the other team to fewer) or defense (hoping to shut out the other team and find the net once) or one that's evenly balanced. Because coaches know they won't have many opportunities to switch between offensive and defensive personnel during the game, they have to come up with a winning lineup and pretty much stick with it.

That's my view of investing. Few people (if any) have the ability to switch tactics to match market conditions on a timely basis. So investors should commit to an approach—hopefully one that will serve them through a variety of scenarios. They can be aggressive, hoping they'll make a lot on the winners and not give it back on the losers. They can emphasize defense, hoping to keep up in good times and excel by losing less than others in bad times. Or they can balance offense and defense, largely giving up on tactical timing but aiming to win through superior security selection in both up and down markets.

Oaktree's preference for defense is clear. In good times, we feel it's okay if we just keep up with the indices (and in the best of times we may even lag a bit). But even average investors make a lot of money in good times, and I doubt many managers get fired for being average in up markets.

///

SETH KLARMAN: *Even if they did, Marks and his partners would certainly prefer to lose the handful of clients who held unrealistic expectations or who didn't care for the Oaktree philosophy than to try to accommodate them. Ultimately, the Oaktree team manages a substantial amount of their own capital, and their approach has the same appeal to them that it should have to investors everywhere.*

\\

Oaktree portfolios are set up to outperform in bad times, and that's when we think outperformance is essential. Clearly, if we can keep up in good times and outperform in bad times, we'll have above-average results over full cycles with below-average volatility, and our clients will enjoy outperformance when others are suffering.

"WHAT'S YOUR GAME PLAN?" SEPTEMBER 5, 2003

What's more important to you: scoring points or keeping your opponent from doing so? In investing, will you go for winners or try to avoid losers? (Or, perhaps more appropriately, how will you balance the two?) Great danger lies in acting without having considered these questions.

And, by the way, there's no right choice between offense and defense. Lots of possible routes can bring you to success, and your decision should be a function of your personality and leanings, the extent of your belief in your ability, and the peculiarities of the markets you work in and the clients you work for.

≈

What is offense in investing, and what is defense? Offense is easy to define. It's the adoption of aggressive tactics and elevated risk in the pursuit of above-average gains. But what's defense? Rather than doing the right thing, the defensive investor's main emphasis is on not doing the wrong thing.

Is there a difference between doing the right thing and avoiding doing the wrong thing? On the surface, they sound quite alike. But when you look deeper, there's a big difference between the mind-set needed for one and the mind-set needed for the other, and a big difference in the tactics to which the two lead.

While defense may sound like little more than trying to avoid bad outcomes, it's not as negative or nonaspirational as that. Defense actually can be seen as an attempt at higher returns, but more through the avoidance of minuses than through the inclusion of pluses, and more through consistent but perhaps moderate progress than through occasional flashes of brilliance.

There are two principal elements in investment defense. The first is the exclusion of losers from portfolios. This is best accomplished by conducting extensive due diligence, applying high standards, demanding a low price and generous margin for error (see later in this chapter) and being less willing to bet on continued prosperity, rosy forecasts and developments that may be uncertain.

The second element is the avoidance of poor years and, especially, exposure to meltdown in crashes. In addition to the ingredients described previously that help keep individual losing investments from the portfolio, this aspect of investment defense requires thoughtful portfolio diversification, limits on the overall riskiness borne, and a general tilt toward safety.

Concentration (the opposite of diversification) and leverage are two examples of offense. They'll add to returns when they work but prove harmful when they don't: again, the potential for higher highs and lower lows from aggressive tactics. Use enough of them, however, and they can jeopardize your investment survival if things go awry. Defense, on the other hand, can increase your likelihood of being able to get through the tough times and survive long enough to enjoy the eventual payoff from smart investments.

JOEL GREENBLATT: *Here is part of the tradeoff with diversification. You must be diversified enough to survive bad times or bad luck so that skill and good process can have the chance to pay off over the long term.*

Investors must brace for untoward developments. There are lots of forms of financial activity that reasonably can be expected to work on average, but they might give you one bad day on which you melt down because of a precarious structure or excess leverage.

But is it really that simple? It's easy to say you should prepare for bad days. But how bad? What's the worst case, and must you be equipped to meet it every day?

Like everything else in investing, this isn't a matter of black and white. The amount of risk you'll bear is a function of the extent to which you choose to pursue return. The amount of safety you build into your portfolio should be based on how much potential return you're willing to forgo. There's no right answer, just trade-offs. That's why I added this concluding thought in December 2007: "Because ensuring the ability to survive under adverse circumstances is incompatible with maximizing returns in the good times, investors must choose between the two."

"THE AVIARY," MAY 16, 2008

～

The critical element in defensive investing is what Warren Buffett calls "margin of safety" or "margin for error." (He seems to go back and forth between the two without making a distinction.) This subject deserves considerable discussion.

JOEL GREENBLATT: *"Margin of safety" and "Mr. Market" are the two ideas that Buffett refers to as Graham's greatest contributions to the investing world.*

It's not hard to make investments that will be successful if the future unfolds as expected. There's little mystery in how to profit under the assumption that the economy will go a certain way and particular industries and companies will do better than others. Tightly targeted investments can be highly successful if the future turns out as you hope.

But you might want to give some thought to how you'll fare if the future doesn't oblige. In short, what is it that makes outcomes tolerable even when the future doesn't live up to your expectations? The answer is *margin for error.*

HOWARD MARKS: *Understanding uncertainty: Despite the presence of uncertainty, many investors try to select the ideal strategy through which to maximize return. But if instead we acknowledge the existence of uncertainty, we should insist on building in a generous margin of safety. That's what keeps your result tolerable when undesirable outcomes materialize.*

Think about what happens when a lender makes a loan. It's not hard to make loans that will be repaid if conditions remain as they are—e.g., if there's no recession and the borrower holds on to his or her job. But what will enable that loan to be repaid even if conditions deteriorate? Once again, margin for error. If the borrower becomes jobless, the probability of the loan being repaid is greater if there are savings, salable assets or alternative sources of income to fall back on. These things provide the lender's margin for error.

The contrast is simple. The lender who insists on margin for error and lends only to strong borrowers will experience few credit losses. But this lender's high standards will cause him or her to forgo lending opportunities that will go to lenders who are less insistent on creditworthiness. The aggressive lender will look smarter than the prudent lender (and make more money) as long as the environment remains salutary.

SETH KLARMAN: *This led one bank executive to comment in 2007 that "as long as the music is playing, you've got to get up and dance" (Citigroup CEO Charles Prince, Financial Times, July 9, 2007). The pressure to manage a company to increase near-term profits while keeping up with industry peers is one of the greatest problems with today's business culture.*

The prudent lender's reward comes only in bad times, in the form of reduced credit losses. The lender who insists on margin for error won't enjoy the highest highs but will also avoid the lowest lows. That's what happens to those who emphasize defense.

CHRISTOPHER DAVIS: *This is a complicated analogy, and I think problematic. In this scenario, what is the incentive for even conservative borrowers to do business with more conservative lenders? The incentive of a rational borrower is to seek the lowest rate without concern for the capability or prudence of the lender.*

Here's another way to illustrate margin for error. You find something you think will be worth $100. If you buy it for $90, you have a good chance of gain, as well as a moderate chance of loss in case your assumptions turn out to be too optimistic. But if you buy it for $70 instead of $90, your chance of loss is less. That $20 reduction provides additional room to be wrong and still come out okay. Low price is the ultimate source of margin for error.

CHRISTOPHER DAVIS: *Also time—for instance, obsolescence risk.*

So the choice is simple: try to maximize returns through aggressive tactics, or build in protection through margin for error. You can't have both in full measure. Will it be offense, defense or a mix of the two (and, if so, in what proportions)?

~

Of the two ways to perform as an investor—racking up exceptional gains and avoiding losses—I believe the latter is the more dependable. Achieving gains usually has something to do with being right about events that are on the come, whereas losses can be minimized by ascertaining that tangible value is present, the herd's expectations are moderate and prices are low. My experience tells me the latter can be done with greater consistency.

A conscious balance must be struck between striving for return and limiting risk—between offense and defense. In fixed income, where I got my start as a portfolio manager, returns are limited and the manager's greatest contribution comes through the avoidance of loss. Because the upside is truly "fixed," the only variability is on the downside, and avoiding it holds the key. Thus, distinguishing yourself as a bond investor isn't a matter of which paying bonds you hold, but largely of whether you're able to exclude bonds that don't pay. According to Graham and Dodd, this emphasis on exclusion makes fixed income investing a *negative art*.

On the other hand, in equities and other more upside-oriented areas, avoiding losses isn't enough; potential for return must be present as well. While the fixed income investor can pretty much practice defense exclusively, the investor who moves beyond fixed income—typically in search of higher return—has to balance offense and defense.

The key is that word *balance*. The fact that investors need offense in addition to defense doesn't mean they should be indifferent to the mix between the two. If investors want to strive for more return, they generally have to take on more uncertainty—more risk. If investors aspire to higher returns than can be achieved in bonds, they can't expect to get there through loss avoidance alone. Some offense is needed, and with offense comes increased uncertainty. A decision to go that way should be made consciously and intelligently.

~

Perhaps more than any other one thing, Oaktree's activities are based on defense. (But not to the exclusion of offense. Not everything we engage in is a negative art. You can't invest successfully in convertibles, distressed debt or real estate if you're not willing to think about both upside *and* downside.)

JOEL GREENBLATT: *Investors think about this tension between risk and reward in conjunction with the probabilities of each. One way to maximize the asymmetry of risk and reward is to make sure you minimize risk. I've said this before in another place: if you minimize the chance of loss in an investment, most of the other alternatives are good.*

Investing is a testosterone-laden world where too many people think about how good they are and how much they'll make if they swing for the fences and connect. Ask some investors of the "I know" school to tell you what makes them good, and you'll hear a lot about home runs they've hit in the past and the home-runs-in-the-making that reside in their current portfolio. How many talk about consistency, or the fact that their worst year wasn't too bad?

One of the most striking things I've noted over the last thirty-five years is how brief most outstanding investment careers are. Not as short as the careers of professional athletes, but shorter than they should be in a physically nondestructive vocation.

Where are the leading competitors from the days when I first managed high yield bonds twenty-five or thirty years ago? Almost none of them are around anymore. And astoundingly, not one of our prominent distressed debt competitors from the early days fifteen or twenty years ago remains a leader today.

Where'd they go? Many disappeared because organizational flaws rendered their game plans unsustainable. And the rest are gone because they swung for the fences but struck out instead.

That brings up something that I consider a great paradox: I don't think many investment managers' careers end because they fail to hit home runs. Rather, they end up out of the game because they strike out too often—not because they don't have enough winners, but because they have too many losers.

CHRISTOPHER DAVIS: *In equities, you can go too far, though—for instance, you can hide in investments perceived to be safe, thus avoiding controversy.*

And yet, lots of managers keep swinging for the fences.

PAUL JOHNSON: *I believe Marks's observation is correct that many money managers are escorted from the business because their investment approach leads to too many failures.*

- They bet too much when they think they have a winning idea or a correct view of the future, concentrating their portfolios rather than diversifying.
- They incur excessive transaction costs by changing their holdings too often or attempting to time the market.
- And they position their portfolios for favorable scenarios and hoped-for outcomes, rather than ensuring that they'll be able to survive the inevitable miscalculation or stroke of bad luck.

At Oaktree, on the other hand, we believe firmly that "if we avoid the losers, the winners will take care of themselves." That's been our motto since the beginning, and it always will be. We go for batting average, not home runs. We know others will get the headlines for their big victories and spectacular seasons. But we expect to be around at the finish because of consistent good performance that produces satisfied clients.

"WHAT'S YOUR GAME PLAN?" SEPTEMBER 5, 2003

Figures 5.1 and 5.2 suggest there are gains to be had for assuming risk. The difference between the two figures, of course, is that the former doesn't indicate the great uncertainty entailed in bearing increased risk, while the latter does. As figure 5.2 makes clear, riskier investments entail wider ranges of outcomes, including the possibility of losses instead of the hoped-for gains.

Playing offense—trying for winners through risk bearing—is a high-octane activity. It might bring the gains you seek . . . or pronounced disappointment. And here's something else to think about: the more challenging and potentially lucrative the waters you fish in, the more likely they are to have attracted skilled fishermen. Unless your skills render you fully competitive, you're more likely to be prey than victor. Playing offense, bearing risk and operating in technically challenging fields mustn't be attempted without the requisite competence.

In addition to technical skills, aggressive investing also requires intestinal fortitude, patient clients (if you manage money for others) and dependable capital. When developments become adverse, you'll need these things to get through. Investment decisions may have the potential to work out in the long run or on average, but without these things, the aggressive investor may not get to see the long run.

Operating a high-risk portfolio is like performing on the high wire without a net. The payoff for success may be high and bring oohs and aahs. But those slipups will kill you.

The bottom line on striving for superior performance has a lot to do with daring to be great. . . . One of the investor's first and most fundamental decisions has to be on the question of how far out the portfolio will venture. How much emphasis should be put on diversifying, avoiding loss and ensuring against below-pack performance, and how much on sacrificing these things in the hope of doing better?

I learned a lot from my favorite fortune cookie: *The cautious seldom err or write great poetry*. It cuts two ways, which makes it thought provoking. Caution can help us avoid mistakes, but it can also keep us from great accomplishments.

Personally, I like caution in money managers. I believe that in many cases, the avoidance of losses and terrible years is more easily achieved than repeated greatness, and thus risk control is more likely to create a solid foundation for a superior long-term track record. Investing scared, requiring good value and a substantial margin for error, and being conscious of what you don't know and can't control are hallmarks of the best investors I know.

"DARE TO BE GREAT," SEPTEMBER 7, 2006

PAUL JOHNSON: *All investors should heed this advice.*

The choice between offense and defense, like so many in this book, defies an easy answer. For example, consider this conundrum: Many people seem unwilling to do enough of anything (e.g., buy a stock, commit to an asset class or invest with a manager) such that it could significantly harm their results if it doesn't work. But in order for something to be able to materially help your return if it succeeds, you have to do enough so that it could materially hurt you if it fails.

HOWARD MARKS: *Fear of looking wrong: This dilemma shows how the fear of looking wrong interferes with implementing judgments and how hard it is to be a successful investor if you're worried about appearances. Investment committees that behave "institutionally" do so for the simple reason that the pain associated with looking wrong is too great to bear. But the bottom line is simple and absolutely true: if you're dominated by an unwillingness to be wrong, you'll never be able to adopt the lonely, contrarian positions required for serious investment success.*

In investing, almost everything is a two-edged sword. That goes for opting to take bigger risks, substituting concentration for diversification and using leverage to magnify gains. The only exception is genuine personal skill. As for all the rest, if it'll help if it works, that means it'll hurt if it doesn't. That's what makes the choice between offense and defense important and challenging.

Many see this decision as the choice between aspiring for more and settling for less. For the thoughtful investor, however, the answer is that defense can provide good returns achieved consistently, while offense may consist of dreams that often go unmet. For me, defense is the way to go.

Investing defensively can cause you to miss out on things that are hot and get hotter, and it can leave you with your bat on your shoulder in trip after trip to the plate. You may hit fewer home runs than another investor . . . but you're also likely to have fewer strikeouts and fewer inning-ending double plays.

Defensive investing sounds very erudite, but I can simplify it: Invest scared!

PAUL JOHNSON: *I love this comment. I have met few investors who invest scared, except, of course, during a general market panic. But even in those cases they are not investing scared: they are no longer investing because they are too scared!*

Worry about the possibility of loss. Worry that there's something you don't know. Worry that you can make high-quality decisions but still be hit by bad luck or surprise events. Investing scared will prevent hubris; will keep your guard up and your mental adrenaline flowing; will make you insist on adequate margin of safety; and will increase the chances that your portfolio is prepared for things going wrong. And if nothing does go wrong, surely the winners will take care of themselves.

"THE MOST IMPORTANT THING," JULY 1, 2003

18

The Most Important Thing Is . . . Avoiding Pitfalls

An investor needs do very few things right as long as he avoids big mistakes.

WARREN BUFFETT

//

PAUL JOHNSON: *The Buffett quotation explains it all.*

\\

In my book, trying to avoid losses is more important than striving for great investment successes. The latter can be achieved some of the time, but the occasional failures may be crippling. The former can be done more often and more dependably . . . and with consequences when it fails that are more tolerable. With a risky portfolio, a downward fluctuation may make you lose faith or be sold out at the low. A portfolio that contains too little risk can make you underperform in a bull market, but no one ever went bust from that; there are far worse fates.

~

To avoid losses, we need to understand and avoid the pitfalls that create them. In this chapter I bring together some of the key issues discussed in earlier chapters, in the hope that highlighting them under one umbrella will help investors become more alert for trouble spots. The starting point consists of realizing that many kinds of pitfalls exist and learning what they look like.

I think of the sources of error as being primarily analytical/intellectual or psychological/emotional. The former are straightforward: we collect too little information or incorrect information. Or perhaps we apply the wrong analytical processes, make errors in our computations or omit ones we should have performed. There are far too many errors of this sort for me to enumerate, and anyway, this book is more about philosophy and mind-set than it is about analytical processes.

One type of analytical error that I do want to spend some time on, however, is what I call "failure of imagination." By that I mean either being unable to conceive of the full range of possible outcomes or not fully understanding the consequences of the more extreme occurrences.

CHRISTOPHER DAVIS: *In other words, errors of quantification versus errors of judgment.*

I go into this subject at greater length in the next section.

Many of the psychological or emotional sources of error were discussed in previous chapters: greed and fear; willingness to suspend disbelief and skepticism; ego and envy; the drive to pursue high returns through risk bearing; and the tendency to overrate one's foreknowledge. These things contribute to booms and busts, in which most investors join together to do exactly the wrong thing.

Another important pitfall—largely psychological, but important enough to constitute its own category—is the failure to recognize market cycles and manias and move in the opposite direction. Extremes in cycles and trends don't occur often, and thus they're not a frequent source of error, but they give rise to the largest errors. The power of herd psychology to compel conformity and capitulation is nearly irresistible, making it essential that investors resist them. These, too, were discussed earlier.

~

"Failure of imagination"—the inability to understand in advance the full breadth of the range of outcomes—is particularly interesting, and it takes effect in many ways.

As I've said before, investing consists entirely of dealing with the future. In order to invest we must have a view of what the future will look like. In general, we have little choice but to assume it will look pretty much like the past. Thus, it's relatively uncommon for anyone to say, "The average price/earnings ratio on U.S. stocks has been 15 over the last fifty years, and I predict that in the coming years it will be 10 (or 20)."

So most investors extrapolate the past into the future—and, in particular, the recent past. Why the recent past? First, many important financial phenomena follow long cycles, meaning those who experience an extreme event often retire or die off before the next recurrence. Second, as John Kenneth Galbraith said, the financial memory tends to be extremely short. And third, any chance of remembering tends to be erased by the promise of easy money that's inevitably a part of the latest investment fad.

Most of the time the future is indeed like the past, so extrapolation doesn't do any harm. But at the important turning points, when the future stops being like the past, extrapolation fails and large amounts of money are either lost or not made.

Thus, it's important to return to Bruce Newberg's pithy observation about the big difference between probability and outcome. Things that aren't supposed to happen do happen. Short-run outcomes can diverge from the long-run probabilities, and occurrences can cluster. For example, double sixes should come up once in every 36 rolls of the dice. But they can come up five times in a row—and never again in the next 175 rolls—and in the long run have occurred as often as they're supposed to.

Relying to excess on the fact that something "should happen" can kill you when it doesn't. Even if you properly understand the underlying probability distribution, you can't count on things happening as they're supposed to. And the success of your investment actions shouldn't be highly dependent on normal outcomes prevailing; instead, you must allow for outliers.

PAUL JOHNSON: *The key to this wisdom is the phrase "you must allow for outliers." Marks is unequivocal in his message.*

Investors make investments only because they expect them to work out, and their analysis will center on the likely scenarios.

SETH KLARMAN: *Similarly, the great majority of sell-side research focuses on a single, most likely scenario and ignores the range of possible outcomes.*

But they mustn't fixate on that which is supposed to happen to the exclusion of the other possibilities . . . and load up on risk and leverage to the point where negative outcomes will do them in. Most of the meltdowns in the recent credit crisis took place because something didn't go as it was supposed to.

The financial crisis occurred largely because never-before-seen events collided with risky, levered structures that weren't engineered to withstand them.

PAUL JOHNSON: *A brilliantly simple explanation of the 2008 credit crisis, and beautifully said.*

For example, mortgage derivatives had been designed and rated on the assumption that there couldn't be a nationwide decline in home prices, since there never had been one (or at least not in the modern era of statistics). But then we had one of major proportions, and structures built on the assumption that it couldn't happen were decimated.

As an aside, it's worth noting that the assumption that something can't happen has the potential to make it happen, since people who believe it can't happen will engage in risky behavior and thus alter the environment. Twenty or more years ago, the term *mortgage lending* was associated inextricably with the word *conservative*. Home buyers put down 20 to 30 percent of the purchase price; mortgage payments were limited to 25 percent of monthly income by tradition; houses were appraised carefully; and borrowers' income and financial position had to be documented. But when the appetite for mortgage-backed securities rose in the past decade—in part because mortgages had always performed so dependably and it was agreed there couldn't be a nationwide surge in mortgage defaults— many of these traditional norms went out the window. The consequences shouldn't have come as a surprise.

That brings me back to a dilemma we have to navigate. How much time and capital should an investor devote to protecting against the improbable disaster? We can insure against every extreme outcome; for example, against both deflation and hyperinflation. But doing so will be costly, and the cost will detract from investment returns when that protection turns out not to have been needed . . . and that'll be most of the time. You could require your portfolio to do well in a rerun of 2008, but then you'd hold only Treasurys, cash and gold. Is that a viable strategy?

Probably not. So the general rule is that it's important to avoid pitfalls, but there must be a limit. And the limit is different for each investor.

There's another important aspect of failure of imagination. Everyone knows assets have prospective returns and risks, and they're possible to guess at. But few people understand asset correlation: how one asset will react to a change in another, or that two assets will react similarly to a change in a third. Understanding and anticipating the power of correlation—and thus the limitations of diversification—is a principal aspect of risk control and portfolio management, but it's very hard to accomplish. The failure to correctly anticipate co-movement within a portfolio is a critical source of investment error.

Investors often fail to appreciate the common threads that run through portfolios. Everyone knows that if one automaker's stock falls, factors they have in common could make all auto stocks decline simultaneously. Fewer people understand the connections that could make all U.S. stocks fall, or all stocks in the developed world, or all stocks worldwide, or all stocks and bonds, etc.

So failure of imagination consists in the first instance of not anticipating the possible extremeness of future events, and in the second instance of failing to understand the knock-on consequences of extreme events.

CHRISTOPHER DAVIS: *This is true.*

In the recent credit crisis, some skeptics may have suspected that subprime mortgages would default in large numbers, but not necessarily that the ramifications would spread far beyond the mortgage market. Few people envisioned the mortgage collapse, but far fewer anticipated that as a result commercial paper and money market funds would be compromised; or that Lehman Brothers, Bear Stearns and Merrill Lynch would cease to exist as independent companies; or that General Motors and Chrysler would file for bankruptcy and require bailouts.

~

In many ways, psychological forces are some of the most interesting sources of investment error. They can greatly influence security prices. When they cause some investors to take an extreme view that isn't balanced out by others, these forces can make prices go way too high or way too low. This is the origin of bubbles and crashes.

How are investors harmed by these forces?

- By succumbing to them
- By participating unknowingly in markets that have been distorted by others' succumbing
- By failing to take advantage when those distortions are present

Are these all the same thing? I don't think so. Let's dissect these three mistakes in the context of one of the most insidious psychological forces: greed.

When greed goes to excess, security prices tend to be too high. That makes prospective return low and risk high. The assets in question represent mistakes waiting to produce loss . . . or to be taken advantage of.

The first of the three errors just listed—succumbing to negative influences—means joining in the greed and buying. If the desire to make money causes you to buy even though price is too high, in the hope that the asset will continue appreciating or the tactic will keep working, you're setting yourself up for disappointment. If you buy when price exceeds intrinsic value, you'll have to be extremely lucky—the asset will have to go from overvalued to even more overvalued—in order to experience gain rather than loss. Certainly the elevated price renders the latter more likely than the former.

The second of the errors is something we might call the error of not noticing. You may not be motivated by greed; for example, your 401(k) plan may invest in the stock market steadily and passively through an index fund. Nevertheless, participating, even unknowingly, in a market that has become elevated because of undisciplined buying by others has serious implications for you.

Each negative influence, and each kind of "wrong" market, presents ways to benefit instead of err. Thus, the third form of error doesn't consist of doing the wrong thing, but rather of failing to do the right thing. Average investors are fortunate if they can avoid pitfalls, whereas superior investors look to take advantage of them. Most investors would hope to not buy, or perhaps even to sell, when greed has driven a stock's price too high. But superior investors might sell it short in order to profit when the price falls. Committing the third form of error—e.g., failing to short an overvalued stock—is a different kind of mistake, an error of omission, but probably one most investors would be willing to live with.

~

As I mentioned before, among the pitfalls attributable to psychology is investors' occasional willingness to accept the novel rationales that underlie bubbles and crashes, usually out of a belief that "it's different this time." In bullish markets, inadequate skepticism makes this a frequent occurrence, as investors accept that

- some new development will change the world,
- patterns that have been the rule in the past (like the ups and downs of the business cycle) will no longer occur,
- the rules have been changed (such as the standards that determine whether companies are creditworthy and their debt worth holding), or
- traditional valuation norms are no longer relevant (including price/ earnings ratios for stocks, yield spreads for bonds or capitalization rates for real estate).

Because of the way the pendulum swings (see chapter 9), these errors often occur simultaneously, when investors become too believing and default on the requirement to be skeptical.

There's always a rational—perhaps even a sophisticated—explanation of why some eighth wonder of the world will work in the investor's favor. However, the explainer usually forgets to mention that (a) the new phenomenon would represent a departure from history, (b) it requires things to go right, (c) many other things could happen instead and (d) many of those might be disastrous.

~

The essential first step in avoiding pitfalls consists of being on the lookout for them. The combination of greed and optimism repeatedly leads people to pursue strategies they hope will produce high returns without high risk; pay elevated prices for securities that are in vogue; and hold things after they have become highly priced in the hope there's still some appreciation left. Afterwards, hindsight shows everyone what went wrong: that expectations were unrealistic and risks were ignored. But learning about pitfalls through painful experience is of only limited help. The key is to try to anticipate them. To illustrate, I turn to the recent credit crisis.

The markets are a classroom where lessons are taught every day. The keys to investment success lie in observing and learning. In December 2007, with the subprime problem well under way and its potential for contagion to other markets in the process of becoming clear, I set out to enumerate the lessons that I thought should be learned from it. By the time I completed that task, I realized that these weren't just the lessons of the latest crisis, but key lessons for all time. While I've touched on many of these elsewhere, you may benefit from seeing them all together in one place.

PAUL JOHNSON: *The lessons to be learned from the 2008 crisis, listed below, are well articulated and brilliantly insightful. Not much more needs to be said on the forces that devastated so many investment portfolios and financial services companies.*

What We Learn from a Crisis—or Ought To

- *Too much capital availability makes money flow to the wrong places.* When capital is scarce and in demand, investors are faced with allocation choices regarding the best use for their capital, and they get to make their decisions with patience and discipline. But when there's too much capital chasing too few ideas, investments will be made that do not deserve to be made.
- *When capital goes where it shouldn't, bad things happen.* In times of capital market stringency, deserving borrowers are turned away. But when money's everywhere, unqualified borrowers are offered money on a silver platter. The inevitable results include delinquencies, bankruptcies and losses.
- *When capital is in oversupply, investors compete for deals by accepting low returns and a slender margin for error.* When people want to buy something, their competition takes the form of an auction in which they bid higher and higher. When you think about it, bidding more for something is the same as saying you'll take less for your money. Thus, the bids for investments can be viewed as a statement of how little return investors demand and how much risk they're willing to accept.

CHRISTOPHER DAVIS: *This is one of the reasons that we always think in terms of earnings yield (which is just the inverse of the P/E) rather than in P/Es; doing so allows for easy comparison to fixed-income alternatives.*

- *Widespread disregard for risk creates great risk.* "Nothing can go wrong." "No price is too high." "Someone will always pay me more for it." "If I don't move quickly, someone else will buy it." Statements like these indicate that risk is being given short shrift. This cycle's version saw people think that because they were buying better companies or financing with more borrower-friendly debt, buyout transactions could support larger and larger amounts of leverage. This caused them to ignore the risk of untoward developments and the danger inherent in highly leveraged capital structures.
- *Inadequate due diligence leads to investment losses.* The best defense against loss is thorough, insightful analysis and insistence on what Warren Buffett calls "margin for error." But in hot markets, people worry about missing out, not about losing money, and time-consuming, skeptical analysis becomes the province of old fogeys.
- *In heady times, capital is devoted to innovative investments, many of which fail the test of time.* Bullish investors focus on what might work, not what might go wrong. Eagerness takes over from prudence, causing people to accept new investment products they don't understand. Later, they wonder what they could have been thinking.
- *Hidden fault lines running through portfolios can make the prices of seemingly unrelated assets move in tandem.* It's easier to assess the return and risk of an investment than to understand how it will move relative to others. Correlation is often underestimated, especially because of the degree to which it increases in crisis. A portfolio may appear to be diversified as to asset class, industry and geography, but in tough times, nonfundamental factors such as margin calls, frozen markets and a general rise in risk aversion can become dominant, affecting everything similarly.

- *Psychological and technical factors can swamp fundamentals.* In the long run, value creation and destruction are driven by fundamentals such as economic trends, companies' earnings, demand for products and the skillfulness of managements. But in the short run, markets are highly responsive to investor psychology and the technical factors that influence the supply and demand for assets. In fact, I think confidence matters more than anything else in the short run. Anything can happen in this regard, with results that are both unpredictable and irrational.

JOEL GREENBLATT: *The market eventually gets it right. In the short term, psychology and technical factors can make the wait for the long term exceptionally painful, but often this is the source of great opportunity.*

- *Markets change, invalidating models.* Accounts of the difficulties of "quant" funds center on the failure of computer models and their underlying assumptions. The computers that run portfolios attempt primarily to profit from patterns that held true in past markets. They can't predict changes in those patterns; they can't anticipate aberrant periods; and thus they generally overestimate the reliability of past norms.

CHRISTOPHER DAVIS: *Or as Buffett has said, "Beware of geeks with models."*

- *Leverage magnifies outcomes but doesn't add value.* It can make great sense to use leverage to increase your investment in assets at bargain prices offering high promised returns or generous risk premiums. But it can be dangerous to use leverage to buy more of assets that offer low returns or narrow risk spreads—in other words, assets that are fully priced or overpriced. It makes little sense to use leverage to try to turn inadequate returns into adequate returns.

PAUL JOHNSON: *The bullet on the role of leverage needs extra emphasis. Too many investors fail to appreciate this wise nugget.*

- *Excesses correct.* When investor psychology is extremely rosy and markets are "priced for perfection"—based on an assumption that things will always be good—the scene is set for capital destruction. It may happen because investors' assumptions turn out to be too optimistic, because negative events occur, or simply because too-high prices collapse of their own weight.

Most of these eleven lessons can be reduced to just one: be alert to what's going on around you with regard to the supply/demand balance for investable funds and the eagerness to spend them. We know what it feels like when there's too little capital around and great hesitance to part with it: worthwhile investments can go begging, and business can slow throughout the economy. It's called a credit crunch. But the opposite deserves to receive no less attention. There's no official term for it, so "too much money chasing too few ideas" may have to do.

Regardless of what it's called, an oversupply of capital and the accompanying dearth of prudence such as we saw in 2004–2007—with their pernicious effects—can be dangerous for your investing health and must be recognized and dealt with.

"NO DIFFERENT THIS TIME," DECEMBER 17, 2007

The global crisis provided a great opportunity to learn, since it entailed so many grave errors and offered up the lessons enumerated in my December 2007 memo. Pitfalls were everywhere: investors were unworried, even ebullient in the years leading up. People believed that risk had been banished, and thus they need worry only about missing opportunity and failing to keep up, not about losing money. Risky, untested investment innovations were adopted on the basis of shaky assumptions. Undue weight was accorded opaque models and "black boxes," financial engineers and "quants," and performance records compiled during salutary periods. Leverage was piled on top of leverage.

HOWARD MARKS: *The riskiest things: A high level of belief and a corresponding low level of skepticism always play a large part in the ascent of prices that, afterward, everyone sees as having risen too high. Buying with borrowed money often increases the*

extent to which prices will become elevated, the likelihood of ensu-
ing disaster, and the extent of the pain when it arrives. These are
among the riskiest things.

Almost no one knew exactly what the consequences would be, but it was possible to have a sense that we were riding for a fall. Even though specific pitfalls may not have been susceptible to identification and avoidance, this was a perfect time to recognize that many were lurking, and thus to adopt a more defensive posture. Failure to do so was the great error of the crisis.

Leading up to it, what could investors have done? The answers lay in

- taking note of the carefree, incautious behavior of others,
- preparing psychologically for a downturn,
- selling assets, or at least the more risk-prone ones,
- reducing leverage,
- raising cash (and returning cash to clients if you invested for others), and
- generally tilting portfolios toward increased defensiveness.

Any of these would have helped. Although almost nothing performed well in the meltdown of 2008, it was possible as a result of elevated caution to lose less than others and reduce the pain. While it was nigh onto impossible to avoid declines completely, relative outperformance in the form of smaller losses was enough to let you do better in the decline and take greater advantage of the rebound.

The crisis was rife with potential pitfalls: first, opportunities to succumb and lose, and then opportunities to go into a shell and miss out. In periods that are relatively loss free, people tend to think of risk as volatility and become convinced they can live with it. If that were true, they would experience markdowns, invest more at the lows and go on to enjoy the recovery, coming out ahead in the long run. But if the ability to live with volatility and maintain one's composure has been overestimated—and usually it has—that error tends to come to light when the market is at its nadir. Loss of confidence and resolve can cause investors to sell at the bottom, converting downward fluctuations into permanent losses and preventing them from participating fully in the subsequent recovery. This is the greatest error in investing—the most unfortunate aspect of pro-cyclical behavior—because of its permanence and because it tends to affect large portions of portfolios.

//

CHRISTOPHER DAVIS: *We experienced this at Davis Advisors in 1975.*

JOEL GREENBLATT: *Investor, know thyself. How much pain can you take on the downside? This should inform the size of your initial portfolio allocations to specific investments and investment categories.*

\\

Since countercyclical behavior was the essential element in avoiding the full effect of the recent crisis, behaving pro-cyclically presented the greatest potential pitfall. Investors who maintained their bullish positions as the market rose (or added to them) were least prepared for the bust and the subsequent recovery.

- The declines had maximum psychological impact.
- Margin calls and confiscations of collateral decimated levered vehicles.
- Troubled holdings required remedial action that occupied managers.
- As usual, the loss of confidence prevented many from doing the right thing at the right time.

While it's true that you can't spend relative outperformance, human nature causes defensive investors and their less traumatized clients to derive comfort in down markets when they lose less than others. This has two very important effects. First, it enables them to maintain their equanimity and resist the psychological pressures that often make people sell at lows. Second, being in a better frame of mind and better financial condition, they are more able to profit from the carnage by buying at lows. Thus, they generally do better in recoveries.

Certainly this is what happened in the last few years. The credit markets were particularly hard-hit in 2007–2008, since they had been the focus of innovation, risk taking and the use of leverage. Correspondingly, their gains in 2009 were the best in their history. Surviving the declines and buying at the resultant lows was a great formula for success—especially relative success—but first it required the avoidance of pitfalls.

◠

The formula for error is simple, but the ways it appears are infinite—far too many to allow enumeration. Here are the usual ingredients:

- data or calculation error in the analytical process leads to incorrect appraisal of value;
- the full range of possibilities or their consequences is underestimated;
- greed, fear, envy, ego, suspension of disbelief, conformity or capitulation, or some combination of these, moves to an extreme;
- as a result, either risk taking or risk avoidance becomes excessive;
- prices diverge significantly from value; and
- investors fail to notice this divergence, and perhaps contribute to its furtherance.

Ideally, astute and prudent second-level thinkers take note of the analytical error as well as the failure of other investors to react appropriately. They detect over- or underpriced assets in the context of too-hot or too-cool markets. They set their course to avoid the mistakes others are making and hopefully take advantage instead. The upshot of investment error is simple to define: prices that differ from intrinsic value. Detecting it and acting on it are less simple.

The fascinating and challenging thing is that the error moves around. Sometimes prices are too high and sometimes they're too low. Sometimes the divergence of price from value affects individual securities or assets and sometimes whole markets—sometimes one market and sometimes another. Sometimes the error lies in doing something and sometimes in not doing it, sometimes in being bullish and sometimes in being bearish.

And, of course, by definition most people go along with the error, since without their concurrence it couldn't exist. Acting in the opposite direction requires the adoption of a contrarian position, with the loneliness and feeling of being wrong that it can bring for long periods.

As with the rest of the tasks discussed in this book, avoiding pitfalls and identifying and acting on error aren't susceptible to rules, algorithms or roadmaps. What I would urge is awareness, flexibility, adaptability and a mind-set that is focused on taking cues from the environment.

One way to improve investment results—which we try hard to apply at Oaktree—is to think about what "today's mistake" might be and try to avoid it.

There are times in investing when the likely mistake consists of:

- not buying,

JOEL GREENBLATT: *It's a big world out there. Good investors don't worry too much about this one.*

- not buying enough,
- not making one more bid in an auction,
- holding too much cash,
- not using enough leverage, or
- not taking enough risk.

I don't think that describes 2004. I've always heard that no one awaiting heart surgery ever complained, "I wish I'd gone to the office more." Well, likewise I don't think anyone in the next few years is going to look back and say, "I wish I'd invested more in 2004."

Rather, I think this year's mistake is going to turn out to be:

- buying too much,
- buying too aggressively,
- making one bid too many,
- using too much leverage, and
- taking too much risk in the pursuit of superior returns.

There are times when the investing errors are of omission: the things you should have done but didn't. Today I think the errors are probably of commission: the things you shouldn't have done but did. There are times for aggressiveness. I think this is a time for caution.

"RISK AND RETURN TODAY," OCTOBER 27, 2004

Finally, it's important to bear in mind that in addition to times when the errors are of commission (e.g., buying) and times when they are of omission (failing to buy), there are times when there's no glaring error. When investor psychology is at equilibrium and fear and greed are balanced, asset prices are likely to be fair relative to value. In that case there may be no compelling action, and it's important to know that, too. When there's nothing particularly clever to do, the potential pitfall lies in insisting on being clever.

CHRISTOPHER DAVIS: *This is a great quote.*

19

The Most Important Thing Is . . . Adding Value

The performance of investors who add value is asymmetrical. The percentage of the market's gain they capture is higher than the percentage of loss they suffer. . . . Only skill can be counted on to add more in propitious environments than it costs in hostile ones. This is the investment asymmetry we seek.

It's not hard to perform in line with the market in terms of risk and return. The trick is to do better than the market: to add value. This calls for superior investment skill, superior insight. So here, near the end of the book, we come around full circle to the first chapter and second-level thinkers possessing exceptional skill.

The purpose of this chapter is to explain what it means for skillful investors to add value. To accomplish that, I'm going to introduce two terms from investment theory. One is *beta*, a measure of a portfolio's relative sensitivity to market movements. The other is *alpha*, which I define as personal investment skill, or the ability to generate performance that is unrelated to movement of the market.

∽

As I mentioned earlier, it's easy to achieve the market return. A passive index fund will produce just that result by holding every security in a given market index in proportion to its equity capitalization. Thus, it mirrors the characteristics—e.g., upside potential, downside risk, beta or volatility, growth, richness or cheapness, quality or lack of same—of the selected index and delivers its return. It epitomizes investing without value added.

Let's say, then, that all equity investors start not with a blank sheet of paper but rather with the possibility of simply emulating an index. They can go out and passively buy a market-weighted amount of each stock in the index, in which case their performance will be the same as that of the index. Or they can try for outperformance through active rather than passive investing.

Active investors have a number of options available to them. First, they can decide to make their portfolio more aggressive or more defensive than the index, either on a permanent basis or in an attempt at market timing. If investors choose aggressiveness, for example, they can increase their portfolios' market sensitivity by overweighting those stocks in the index that typically fluctuate more than the rest, or by utilizing leverage. Doing these things will increase the "systematic" riskiness of a portfolio, its beta. (However, theory says that while this may increase a portfolio's return, the return differential will be fully explained by the increase in systematic risk borne. Thus doing these things won't improve the portfolio's risk-adjusted return.)

Second, investors can decide to deviate from the index in order to exploit their stock-picking ability—buying more of some stocks in the index, underweighting or excluding others, and adding some stocks that aren't part of the index. In doing so they will alter the exposure of their portfolios to specific events that occur at individual companies, and thus to price movements that affect only certain stocks, not the whole index. As the composition of their portfolios diverges from the index for "nonsystematic" (we might say "idiosyncratic") reasons, their return will deviate as well. In the long run, however, unless the investors have superior insight, these deviations will cancel out, and their risk-adjusted performance will converge with that of the index.

Active investors who don't possess the superior insight described in chapter 1 are no better than passive investors, and their portfolios shouldn't be expected to perform better than a passive portfolio. They can try hard, put their emphasis on offense or defense, or trade up a storm, but their risk-adjusted performance shouldn't be expected to be better than the passive portfolio. (And it could be worse due to nonsystematic risks borne and transaction costs that are unavailing.)

That doesn't mean that if the market index goes up 15 percent, every non-value-added active investor should be expected to achieve a 15 percent return.

They'll all hold different active portfolios, and some will perform better than others . . . just not consistently or dependably. Collectively they'll reflect the composition of the market, but each will have its own peculiarities.

Pro-risk, aggressive investors, for example, should be expected to make more than the index in good times and lose more in bad times. This is where beta comes in. By the word *beta*, theory means relative volatility, or the relative responsiveness of the portfolio return to the market return. A portfolio with a beta above 1 is expected to be more volatile than the reference market, and a beta below 1 means it'll be less volatile. Multiply the market return by the beta and you'll get the return that a given portfolio should be expected to achieve, omitting nonsystematic sources of risk. If the market is up 15 percent, a portfolio with a beta of 1.2 should return 18 percent (plus or minus alpha).

Theory looks at this information and says the increased return is explained by the increase in beta, or systematic risk. It also says returns don't increase to compensate for risk other than systematic risk. Why don't they? According to theory, the risk that markets compensate for is the risk that is intrinsic and inescapable in investing: systematic or "non-diversifiable" risk. The rest of risk comes from decisions to hold individual stocks: non-systematic risk. Since that risk can be eliminated by diversifying, why should investors be compensated with additional return for bearing it?

According to theory, then, the formula for explaining portfolio performance (y) is as follows:

$$y = \alpha + \beta x$$

Here α is the symbol for alpha, β stands for beta, and x is the return of the market. The market-related return of the portfolio is equal to its beta times the market return, and alpha (skill-related return) is added to arrive at the total return (of course, theory says there's no such thing as alpha).

Although I dismiss the identity between risk and volatility, I insist on considering a portfolio's return in the light of its overall riskiness, as discussed earlier.

CHRISTOPHER DAVIS: *But is beta the right measure of risk? This seems to run a bit counter to the earlier discussion of risk. But even if beta is not the most meaningful or relevant measure, it is certain that Oaktree has done a wonderful job on a risk-adjusted basis.*

A manager who earned 18 percent with a risky portfolio isn't necessarily superior to one who earned 15 percent with a lower-risk portfolio. Risk-adjusted return holds the key, even though—since risk other than volatility can't be quantified—I feel it is best assessed judgmentally, not calculated scientifically.

JOEL GREENBLATT: *Such an important concept for business students (who have likely been taught otherwise)!*

Of course, I also dismiss the idea that the alpha term in the equation has to be zero. Investment skill exists, even though not everyone has it. Only through thinking about risk-adjusted return might we determine whether an investor possesses superior insight, investment skill or alpha . . . that is, whether the investor adds value.

The alpha/beta model is an excellent way to assess portfolios, portfolio managers, investment strategies and asset allocation schemes. It's really an organized way to think about how much of the return comes from what the environment provides and how much from the manager's value added. For example, it's obvious that this manager doesn't have any skill:

Period	Benchmark Return	Portfolio Return
1	10	10
2	6	6
3	0	0
4	−10	−10
5	20	20

But neither does this manager (who moves just half as much as the benchmark):

Period	Benchmark Return	Portfolio Return
1	10	5
2	6	3
3	0	0
4	−10	−5
5	20	10

Or this one (who moves twice as much):

Period	Benchmark Return	Portfolio Return
1	10	20
2	6	12
3	0	0
4	−10	−20
5	20	40

This one has a little:

Period	Benchmark Return	Portfolio Return
1	10	11
2	6	8
3	0	−1
4	−10	−9
5	20	21

While this one has a lot:

Period	Benchmark Return	Portfolio Return
1	10	12
2	6	10
3	0	3
4	−10	2
5	20	30

This one has a ton, if you can live with the volatility:

Period	Benchmark Return	Portfolio Return
1	10	25
2	6	20
3	0	−5
4	−10	−20
5	20	25

What's clear from these tables is that "beating the market" and "superior investing" can be far from synonymous—see years one and two in the third example. It's not just your return that matters, but also what risk you took to get it.

"RETURNS AND HOW THEY GET THAT WAY," NOVEMBER 11, 2002

∾

It's important to keep these considerations in mind when assessing an investor's skill and when comparing the record of a defensive investor and an aggressive investor. You might call this process *style adjusting.*

In a bad year, defensive investors lose less than aggressive investors. Did they add value? Not necessarily. In a good year, aggressive investors make more than defensive investors. Did they do a better job? Few people would say yes without further investigation.

A single year says almost nothing about skill, especially when the results are in line with what would be expected on the basis of the investor's style. It means relatively little that a risk taker achieves a high return in a rising market, or that a conservative investor is able to minimize losses in a decline. The real question is how they do in the long run and in climates for which their style is ill suited.

A two-by-two matrix tells the story.

	Aggressive Investor	Defensive Investor
Without Skill	Gains a lot when the market goes up, and loses a lot when the market goes down	Doesn't lose much when the market goes down, but doesn't gain much when the market goes up
With Skill	Gains a lot when the market goes up, but doesn't lose to the same degree when the market goes down	Doesn't lose much when the market goes down, but captures a fair bit of the gain when the market goes up

The key to this matrix is the symmetry or asymmetry of the performance. Investors who lack skill simply earn the return of the market and the dictates of their style. Without skill, aggressive investors move a lot in both directions, and defensive investors move little in either direction. These investors contribute nothing beyond their choice of style. Each does well when his or her style is in favor but poorly when it isn't.

On the other hand, the performance of investors who add value is asymmetrical. The percentage of the market's gain they capture is higher than the percentage of loss they suffer. Aggressive investors with skill do well in bull markets but don't give it all back in corresponding bear markets, while defensive investors with skill lose relatively little in bear markets but participate reasonably in bull markets.

Everything in investing is a two-edged sword and operates symmetrically, with the exception of superior skill. Only skill can be counted on to add more in propitious environments than it costs in hostile ones. This is the investment asymmetry we seek. Superior skill is *the* prerequisite for it.

JOEL GREENBLATT: *Once again, finding the skilled investor comes down to understanding investment process, not merely assessing recent returns.*

Here's how I describe Oaktree's performance aspirations:

In good years in the market, it's good enough to be average. Everyone makes money in the good years, and I have yet to hear anyone explain convincingly why it's important to beat the market when the market does well. No, in the good years average is good enough.

There is a time, however, when we consider it essential to beat the market, and that's in the bad years. Our clients don't expect to bear the full brunt of market losses when they occur, and neither do we.

Thus, it's our goal to do as well as the market when it does well and better than the market when it does poorly. At first blush that may sound like a modest goal, but it's really quite ambitious.

In order to stay up with the market when it does well, a portfolio has to incorporate good measures of beta and correlation with the market. But if we're aided by beta and correlation on the way up, shouldn't they be expected to hurt us on the way down?

If we're consistently able to decline less when the market declines and also participate fully when the market rises, this can be attributable to only one thing: alpha, or skill.

That's an example of value-added investing, and if demonstrated over a period of decades, it has to come from investment skill.

JOEL GREENBLATT: *However, unlike Oaktree, many investment firms raise a large amount of assets as a result of a good long-term record. With more capital, managers are often forced to invest differently than they did when they were building their great track record. Oaktree actually returns capital whenever the opportunity set shrinks. Few investment firms follow this path.*

Asymmetry—better performance on the upside than on the downside relative to what your style alone would produce—should be every investor's goal.

20

The Most Important Thing Is …
Reasonable Expectations

Return expectations must be reasonable. Anything else
will get you into trouble, usually through the acceptance
of greater risk than is perceived.

I want to point out that no investment activity is likely to be successful
unless the return goal is (a) explicit and (b) reasonable in the absolute and
relative to the risk entailed. Every investment effort should begin with a
statement of what you're trying to accomplish. The key questions are what
your return goal is, how much risk you can tolerate, and how much liquidity you're likely to require in the interim.

≈

Return goals must be reasonable. What returns can we aspire to? Most of
the time—although not necessarily at any particular point in time (and
not necessarily today)—it's reasonable to aspire to returns in single digits
or perhaps low double digits. High teens are something very special, and
anything more should be viewed as the province of experienced pros (and
only the best of those). The same is true of particularly consistent results.
Expecting too much in these regards is likely to lead to disappointment or
loss. There's just one antidote: asking whether the result you're expecting is
too good to be true. This requires the application of skepticism, a quality
that's absolutely essential for investment success.

I don't think normal risk bearing and the normal functioning of the capital markets should be expected to produce returns greater than those just described. Higher returns are "unnatural," and their achievement requires some combination of the following:

- an extremely depressed environment in which to buy (hopefully to be followed by a good environment in which to sell),
- extraordinary investment skill,
- extensive risk bearing,
- heavy leverage, or
- good luck.

Thus, investors should pursue such returns only if they believe some of these elements are present and are willing to stake money on that belief. However, each of these is problematic in some way. Great buying opportunities don't come along every day. Exceptional skill is rare by definition. Risk bearing works against you when things go amiss. So does leverage, which operates in both directions, magnifying losses as well as gains. And certainly luck can't be counted on. Skill is the least ephemeral of these elements, but it's rare (and even skill can't be counted on to produce high returns in a low-return environment).

≈

There are occasional demonstrations of the importance of reasonable expectations, and none is more dramatic than the recent Madoff scandal.

Bernard Madoff perpetrated the greatest Ponzi scheme ever to come to light. He got away with it primarily because his investors failed to question whether his purported accomplishment was feasible.

The returns Madoff claimed weren't outrageously high: just 10 percent a year or so. What was extraordinary was the way he reported them year in and year out. Even a down month was a rarity. Yet few of his investors asked how these returns were achieved or wondered whether they were actually possible.

For most of the twentieth century, common stocks averaged a 10 percent return. But they did it with substantial volatility and a fair number of down years. In fact, while 10 percent was the average, individual-year returns were only rarely within a few percentage points of that figure. History shows equity returns to be highly variable.

If it's dependable returns you're after, you can get them from Treasury bills without subjecting yourself to price volatility, credit risk, inflation risk, or illiquidity. But the returns on T-bills historically have been in low single digits.

How could Madoff have produced the much higher returns of stocks with the dependability of T-bills? Which of the five elements listed above might he have possessed?

- He reported those returns for almost twenty years, regardless of the investment environment.
- No one understood him to possess particular investment skill, and if there was something exceptional about his computer model, what kept others from discovering it and emulating it?
- He claimed not to base his efforts on predicting the direction of the market or picking individual stocks.
- His avowed approach didn't involve leverage.
- No one can be that lucky that long.

There simply was no rational explanation for Madoff's returns. His investors could say either "I checked it out" or "I think it makes sense," but it was impossible to say "I checked it out, and it makes sense." His method and results were simply unsupportable: there weren't enough options outstanding to accommodate the capital he managed, and even if there were, the strategy he described couldn't produce the virtual absence of losing months he claimed. But people regularly suspend disbelief and accept unreasonable expectations when they're told free money is available. The Madoff scandal is an exceptional example of the importance of saying "too good to be true" to return expectations that are unreasonable. But few people seem capable of doing so.

While on the subject of Madoff, I want to mention a good way to sort out the reasonable from the unreasonable. In addition to "Is it too good to be true," just ask "Why me?" When the salesman on the phone offers you a guaranteed route to profit, you should wonder what made him offer it to you rather than hog it for himself. Likewise, but a little more subtly, if an economist or strategist offers a sure-to-be-right view of the future, you should wonder why he or she is still working for a living, since derivatives can be used to turn correct forecasts into vast profits without requiring much capital.

~

Everyone wants to know how to make the correct judgments that can lead to investment success, and lately people have been asking me, "How can you be sure you're investing at the bottom rather than too soon?" Finding the bottom is one of the things about which our expectations have to be reasonable. My answer is simple: "You can't."

"The bottom" is the point at which the price of an asset stops going down and gets ready to start going up. It can be identified only in retrospect.

If markets were rational, such that nothing would sell for less than its "fair value," we could say the bottom has been reached when the price arrives at that point. But since markets overshoot all the time—and price declines continue long after they should have stopped at fair value—there's no way to know when the price has reached a level below which it won't go. It's essential to understand that "cheap" is far from synonymous with "not going to fall further."

I try to look at it logically. There are three times to buy an asset that has been declining: on the way down, at the bottom, or on the way up. I don't believe we ever know when the bottom has been reached, and even if we did, there might not be much for sale there.

If we wait until the bottom has been passed and the price has started to rise, the rising price often causes others to buy, just as it emboldens holders and discourages them from selling. Supply dries up and it becomes hard to buy in size. The would-be buyer finds it's too late.

That leaves buying on the way down, which we should be glad to do. The good news is that if we buy while the price is collapsing, that fact alone often causes others to hide behind the excuse that "it's not our job to catch falling knives." After all, it's when knives are falling that the greatest bargains are available.

There's an important saying attributed to Voltaire: "The perfect is the enemy of the good." This is especially applicable to investing, where insisting on participating only when conditions are perfect—for example, buying only at the bottom—can cause you to miss out on a lot. Perfection in investing is generally unobtainable; the best we can hope for is to make a lot of good investments and exclude most of the bad ones.

How does Oaktree resolve the question of knowing when to buy? We give up on trying to attain perfection or ascertain when the bottom has been reached. Rather, if we think something is cheap, we buy. If it gets cheaper, we buy more. And if we commit all our capital, we assume we'll be able to raise more.

One of the six tenets of our investment philosophy calls for "disavowal of market timing." Yet we expend a lot of effort to diagnose the market environment, and we certainly don't invest regardless of what we think the environment implies for risk and return. Rather, our disinterest in market timing means—above all else—that if we find something attractive, we never say, "It's cheap today, but we think it'll be cheaper in six months, so we'll wait." It's just not realistic to expect to be able to buy at the bottom.

∾

In addition to an excess of trust and shortage of risk consciousness, I think unrealistic expectations played a leading role in creating the recent financial crisis and the ensuing market crash.

Here's how I imagine the attitude toward return of a typical investor—both individual and institutional—in 2005 through 2007:

> I need 8 percent. I'd be glad to earn 10 percent instead. Twelve percent would be even better. Fifteen percent would be great. Twenty percent would be terrific. And 30 percent would be out of this world.

Most people see nothing wrong in this imaginary monologue. But something is very wrong . . . because the investor has failed to ask (a) whether a given goal is reasonable and (b) what would have to be done to achieve it. The truth is that trying for higher returns in a given environment usually requires some increase in risk taking: riskier stocks or bonds, greater portfolio concentration, or increased leverage.

What that typical investor should have said is something like this:

> I need 8 percent. I'd be glad to earn 10 percent instead. Twelve percent would be even better. But I won't try for more than that, because doing so would entail risks I'm just not willing to bear. I don't need 20 percent.

I encourage you to think about "good-enough returns." It's essential to realize that there are returns so high that they aren't worth going for and risks that aren't worth taking.

~

Investment expectations must be reasonable. Anything else will get you into trouble, usually through the acceptance of greater risk than is perceived. Before you swallow the promise of sky-high returns without risk or of steady "absolute returns" at levels much higher than T-bills, you should wonder skeptically whether they're really achievable and not simply alluring; how an investor with your skill can reasonably expect to achieve them; and why an opportunity so potentially lucrative is available to you, ostensibly cheaply. In other words, are they too good to be true?

21

The Most Important Thing Is . . .
Pulling It All Together

The best foundation for a successful investment—or a successful investment career—is value. You must have a good idea of what the thing you're considering buying is worth. There are many components to this and many ways to look at it. To oversimplify, there's cash on the books and the value of the tangible assets; the ability of the company or asset to generate cash; and the potential for these things to increase.

PAUL JOHNSON: *All of the snippets offered in this chapter are worth reading and remembering. This chapter is an excellent recap of the book and the one chapter investors should make a point of rereading regularly.*

~

To achieve superior investment results, your insight into value has to be superior. Thus you must learn things others don't, see things differently or do a better job of analyzing them—ideally, all three.

~

Your view of value has to be based on a solid factual and analytical foundation, and it has to be held firmly. Only then will you know when to buy or sell. Only a strong sense of value will give you the discipline needed to take profits on a highly appreciated asset that everyone thinks will rise nonstop, or the guts to hold and average down in a crisis even as prices go lower every day. Of course, for your efforts in these regards to be profitable, your estimate of value has to be on target.

~

The relationship between price and value holds the ultimate key to investment success. Buying below value is the most dependable route to profit. Paying above value rarely works out as well.

> **JOEL GREENBLATT:** *This is the foundational principle behind all good investing.*

~

What causes an asset to sell below its value? Outstanding buying opportunities exist primarily because perception understates reality. Whereas high quality can be readily apparent, it takes keen insight to detect cheapness. For this reason, investors often mistake objective merit for investment opportunity. The superior investor never forgets that the goal is to find good buys, not good assets.

~

In addition to giving rise to profit potential, buying when price is below value is a key element in limiting risk. Neither paying up for high growth nor participating in a "hot" momentum market can do the same.

~

The relationship between price and value is influenced by psychology and technicals, forces that can dominate fundamentals in the short run.

Extreme swings in price due to those two factors provide opportunities for big profits or big mistakes. To have it be the former rather than the latter, you must stick with the concept of value and cope with psychology and technicals.

~

Economies and markets cycle up and down. Whichever direction they're going at the moment, most people come to believe that they'll go that way forever. This thinking is a source of great danger since it poisons the markets, sends valuations to extremes, and ignites bubbles and panics that most investors find hard to resist.

~

Likewise, the psychology of the investing herd moves in a regular, pendulum-like pattern—from optimism to pessimism; from credulousness to skepticism; from fear of missing opportunity to fear of losing money; and thus from eagerness to buy to urgency to sell. The swing of the pendulum causes the herd to buy at high prices and sell at low prices. Thus, being part of the herd is a formula for disaster, whereas contrarianism at the extremes will help to avert losses and lead eventually to success.

~

In particular, risk aversion—an appropriate amount of which is *the* essential ingredient in a rational market—is sometimes in short supply and sometimes excessive. The fluctuation of investor psychology in this regard plays a very important part in the creation of market bubbles and crashes.

~

The power of psychological influences must never be underestimated. Greed, fear, suspension of disbelief, conformism, envy, ego and capitulation are all part of human nature, and their ability to compel action is profound, especially when they're at extremes and shared by the herd. They'll influence others, and the thoughtful investor will feel them as well. None of us should expect to be immune and insulated from them. Although we will feel them, we must not succumb; rather, we must recognize them for what they are and stand against them. Reason must overcome emotion.

∾

Most trends—both bullish and bearish—eventually become overdone, profiting those who recognize them early but penalizing the last to join. That's the reasoning behind my number one investment adage: "What the wise man does in the beginning, the fool does in the end." The ability to resist excesses is rare, but it's an important attribute of the most successful investors.

∾

It's impossible to know when an overheated market will turn down, or when a downturn will cease and appreciation will take its place. But while we never know where we're going, we ought to know where we are. We can infer where markets stand in their cycle from the behavior of those around us. When other investors are unworried, we should be cautious; when investors are panicked, we should turn aggressive.

∾

Not even contrarianism, however, will produce profits all the time. The great opportunities to buy and sell are associated with valuation extremes, and by definition they don't occur every day. We're bound to also buy and sell at less compelling points in the cycle, since few of us can be content to act only once every few years. We must recognize when the odds are less in our favor and tread more carefully.

∾

Buying based on strong value, low price relative to value, and depressed general psychology is likely to provide the best results. Even then, however, things can go against us for a long time before turning as we think they should. *Underpriced* is far from synonymous with *going up soon*. Thus the importance of my second key adage: "Being too far ahead of your time is indistinguishable from being wrong." It can require patience and fortitude to hold positions long enough to be proved right.

∾

In addition to being able to quantify value and pursue it when it's priced right, successful investors must have a sound approach to the subject of risk. They have to go well beyond the academics' singular definition of risk as volatility and understand that the risk that matters most is the risk of permanent loss. They have to reject increased risk bearing as a surefire formula for investment success and know that riskier investments entail a wider range of possible outcomes and a higher probability of loss. They have to have a sense for the loss potential that's present in each investment and be willing to bear it only when the reward is more than adequate.

~

Most investors are simplistic, preoccupied with the chance for return. Some gain further insight and learn that it's as important to understand risk as it is return. But it's the rare investor who achieves the sophistication required to appreciate correlation, a key element in controlling the riskiness of an overall portfolio. Because of differences in correlation, individual investments of the same absolute riskiness can be combined in different ways to form portfolios with widely varying total risk levels. Most investors think diversification consists of holding many different things; few understand that diversification is effective only if portfolio holdings can be counted on to respond differently to a given development in the environment.

~

While aggressive investing can produce exciting results when it goes right—especially in good times—it's unlikely to generate gains as reliably as defensive investing. Thus, a low incidence and severity of loss is part of most outstanding investment records. Oaktree's motto, "If we avoid the losers, the winners will take care of themselves," has served well over the years. A diversified portfolio of investments, each of which is unlikely to produce significant loss, is a good start toward investment success.

~

Risk control lies at the core of defensive investing. Rather than just trying to do the right thing, the defensive investor places a heavy emphasis on not doing the wrong thing. Because ensuring the ability to survive under adverse circumstances is incompatible with maximizing returns in good times, investors must decide what balance to strike between the two. The defensive investor chooses to emphasize the former.

~

Margin for error is a critical element in defensive investing. Whereas most investments will be successful if the future unfolds as hoped, it takes margin for error to render outcomes tolerable when the future doesn't oblige. An investor can obtain margin for error by insisting on tangible, lasting value in the here and now; buying only when price is well below value; eschewing leverage; and diversifying. Emphasizing these elements can limit your gains in good times, but it will also maximize your chances of coming through intact when things don't go well. My third favorite adage is "Never forget the six-foot-tall man who drowned crossing the stream that was five feet deep on average." Margin for error gives you staying power and gets you through the low spots.

~

Risk control and margin for error should be present in your portfolio at all times. But you must remember that they're "hidden assets." Most years in the markets are good years, but it's only in the bad years—when the tide goes out—that the value of defense becomes evident. Thus, in the good years, defensive investors have to be content with the knowledge that their gains, although perhaps less than maximal, were achieved with risk protection in place . . . even though it turned out not to be needed.

~

One of the essential requirements for investment success—and thus part of most great investors' psychological equipment—is the realization that we don't know what lies ahead in terms of the macro future. Few people if any know more than the consensus about what's going to happen to the economy, interest rates and market aggregates. Thus, the investor's time is better spent trying to gain a knowledge advantage regarding "the knowable": industries, companies and securities. The more micro your focus, the greater the likelihood you can learn things others don't.

∼

Many more investors assume they have knowledge of the future direction of economies and markets—and act that way—than actually do. They take aggressive actions predicated on knowing what's coming, and that rarely produces the desired results. Investing on the basis of strongly held but incorrect forecasts is a source of significant potential loss.

∼

Many investors—amateurs and professionals alike—assume the world runs on orderly processes that can be mastered and predicted. They ignore the randomness of things and the probability distribution that underlies future developments. Thus, they opt to base their actions on the one scenario they predict will unfold. This works sometimes—winning kudos for the investor—but not consistently enough to produce long-term success. In both economic forecasting and investment management, it's worth noting that there's usually someone who gets it exactly right . . . but it's rarely the same person twice. The most successful investors get things "about right" most of the time, and that's much better than the rest.

∼

An important part of getting it right consists of avoiding the pitfalls that are frequently presented by economic fluctuations, companies' travails, the markets' manic swings, and other investors' gullibility. There's no surefire way to accomplish this, but awareness of these potential dangers certainly represents the best starting point for an effort to avoid being victimized by them.

∼

Another essential element is having reasonable expectations. Investors often get into trouble by acting on promises of returns that are unreasonably high or dependable, and by overlooking the fact that, usually, every increase in return pursued is accompanied by an increase in risk borne. The key is to think long and hard about propositions that may be too good to be true.

⁓

Neither defensive investors who limit their losses in a decline nor aggressive investors with substantial gains in a rising market have proved they possess skill. For us to conclude that investors truly add value, we have to see how they perform in environments to which their style isn't particularly well suited. Can the aggressive investor keep from giving back gains when the market turns down? Will the defensive investor participate substantially when the market rises? This kind of asymmetry is the expression of real skill. Does an investor have more winners than losers? Are the gains on the winners bigger than the losses on the losers? Are the good years more beneficial than the bad years are painful? And are the long-term results better than the investor's style alone would suggest? These things are the mark of the superior investor. Without them, returns may be the result of little more than market movement and beta.

⁓

Only investors with unusual insight can regularly divine the probability distribution that governs future events and sense when the potential returns compensate for the risks that lurk in the distribution's negative left-hand tail.

HOWARD MARKS: *Understanding uncertainty: The sentence above does a good job of describing what it takes to deal with uncertainty: a feeling for the things that can happen, the relative likelihood of each, and whether an asset's price (and thus the potential for gains from that price) provides adequate potential reward for bearing the uncertainty that is present.*

This simple description of the requirements for successful investing—based on understanding the range of possible gains and the risk of untoward developments—captures the elements that should receive your attention. I commend the task to you. It'll take you on a challenging, exciting and thought-provoking journey.

JOEL GREENBLATT: *A good understanding of value and how to think about price movements is the key to successful investing. While there are many smart people who can master the estimation of value (especially if they are disciplined enough to stay within what Buffett calls their "circle of competence"), most investors fall short in the area of contextualizing market and individual security price movements. This is where the lessons from Marks's book are so essential. So please feel free to read this chapter (and the entire book!) again and again—a true investment classic.*

About the Contributors

CHRISTOPHER C. DAVIS has more than twenty years of experience in investment management and securities research. He is a portfolio manager of the Davis Large Cap Value portfolios and a member of the research team of other portfolios. Davis joined the firm in 1989. He received his M.A. from the University of St. Andrews in Scotland.

JOEL GREENBLATT is a managing partner of Gotham Capital, a hedge fund that he founded in 1985. He has been a professor since 1996 on the adjunct faculty of Columbia Business School, where he teaches value and special-situation investing. Greenblatt is the former chairman of the board of Alliant Techsystems, a NYSE-listed aerospace and defense company. He is the author of three books: *The Big Secret for the Small Investor* (Crown Business, 2011), *The Little Book That Beats the Market* (John Wiley & Sons, 2005) and *You Can Be a Stock Market Genius* (Simon & Schuster, 1997). Greenblatt holds a B.S. and an M.B.A from the Wharton School.

BRUCE C. GREENWALD holds the Robert Heilbrunn Professorship of Finance and Asset Management at Columbia Business School and is the academic director of the Heilbrunn Center for Graham and Dodd Investing. Since 2007 Greenwald has also served as director of research for First Eagle Funds, a division of Arnhold and S. Bleichroeder Advisers, L.L.C. Greenwald is the author of several books, including *Competition Demystified: A Radically Simplified Approach to Business Strategy* (with Judd Kahn, Putnam Penguin, 2005), and *Value Investing: From Graham to Buffett and Beyond* (with Judd Kahn et al, Wiley, 2001). Greenwald has received a B.S. and a Ph.D. from the Massachusetts Institute of Technology, and an M.P.A. and M.S. from Princeton University.

PAUL JOHNSON founded Nicusa Capital, a fundamentally driven value-oriented long–short hedge fund, in January 2003, and has more than twenty-five years of experience as an investment professional. As an adjunct professor of finance at the Graduate School of Business, Columbia University, Johnson has taught twenty courses since 1992 on securities analysis and value investing to more than six hundred students. He has an M.B.A. in finance from the Executive Program at the Wharton School of the University of Pennsylvania, and a B.A. in economics from the University of California, Berkeley.

SETH A. KLARMAN is the president of The Baupost Group, L.L.C., which currently manages approximately $23 billion on behalf of individual and institutional clients. He has been with the company since its inception in 1982. Author of *Margin of Safety* (Harper-Collins, 1991), a book that outlines his value investment philosophy, Klarman was chosen as lead editor for *Security Analysis*, Sixth Edition (McGraw-Hill, 2008) and has been featured in a variety of investment industry publications. He is a 1982 graduate of Harvard Business School, where he was a Baker Scholar, and received his B.A. in economics from Cornell University in 1979.